MOON POWER

To my dear friend and fellow homeopath, Kate, who got me through our final year of college with a much-needed mixture of laughter, wisdom and chocolate, although not necessarily in that order.

Published in 2021 by Red Wheel Books
An imprint of Red Wheel/Weiser, LLC
with offices at:
65 Parker Street, Suite 7
Newburyport, MA 01950
www.redwheelweiser.com

ISBN 978-1-59003-534-4

10 9 8 7 6 5 4 3 2 1

Printed in Spain

MOON POWER

Jane Struthers

Red Wheel

CONTENTS

Introduction

Would you like to get to know your Moon sign?
Even if you don't know anything else about astrology,
discovering the sign that the Moon occupied when
you were born will give you tremendous insights into
your personality and your path through life. It may
even answer questions about yourself that have always
puzzled you.

The Sun and Moon are the two most important heavenly bodies in the
natal horoscope. Most of us already know quite a lot about our Sun sign
(sometimes referred to as our star sign), but we can be in the dark when it
comes to our Moon sign. If we know about our Sun sign but not our Moon
sign, it's like getting only a small glimpse of a much bigger picture. The
Moon explains so much about us – our habits, our instincts and the areas
of life with which we're most comfortable. It can also explain why
sometimes our Sun sign doesn't tell the whole story about us. For instance,
you might have been born with the Sun in Cancer yet be much more
emotionally cool than most Cancerians. Why is that? Maybe it's because
your Moon is in the detached sign of Aquarius or the reserved sign of
Capricorn. Aha! Suddenly it all makes much more sense.

As well as telling you about your natal Moon, this book will also help you
to understand the effects of the Moon as it passes through each zodiac
sign each month. Tracking the Moon in this way will enable you to get a
greater understanding of the mood and emotional weather that each day
brings, and will also tell you when the best times are to take action – and
when it's wiser to hold tight and wait. Whether you want to know when to
make a serious investment, get involved in a negotiation, embark on a
new partnership, apply for a new job, clear the air with someone, get a new
pet, buy a tempting addition to your wardrobe, plant some flowers or do
many of the other activities that form an intrinsic part of life, this book will
show you how to get your timing right for the best possible results.

All you need to know is your date of birth. The Moon sign calculator in this book will show you how to discover the sign that the Moon occupied when you were born. Knowing your Moon sign is like being given the key to a special astrological lock, because it will reveal so much about your emotions and the things in life that feel most familiar to you. Equipped with this knowledge, you'll be able to read about the powerful combination of your Sun and Moon signs, and also how your Moon sign gets on with the other eleven Moon signs. You could be in for a quite a surprise!

Following the path of the Moon through the skies each month is nothing new. Humans have been doing it for millennia, and we can still see the evidence of that in stone circles such as the UK's Stonehenge, which is thought to be a gigantic calendar that not only tracks the new and full moons but also eclipses. Some of the world's traditional calendars are still governed by the relationship between the Sun and the Moon – in other words, by the cycle of new and full moons. One example is the traditional Chinese calendar, with the Chinese New Year always beginning with the new moon in Aquarius. If you like to celebrate Easter Sunday with a few chocolate eggs, you might be interested to know that this festival is also lunisolar, because Easter is what's known as a 'movable feast' and falls on the first Sunday after the full moon in Libra.

As you'll discover on the following pages, the Moon's cycles affect us biologically as well as emotionally. You'll soon realize that, even in our technological age, where science is sometimes thought to be supreme, the mysterious and beautiful Moon still has a powerful influence on us, not only in terms of our personalities but also in the way that our daily lives unfold.

THE MOON'S MOVEMENTS

We've come a long way from the humorous idea that the Moon is made of cheese, but what do we really know about it? If you've ever wondered what's going on astronomically at new and full moons, or whether it's true that the Moon can affect life on Earth, this part of the book will enlighten you. This information will help you to appreciate the Moon in new ways, so that when you work with the Moon in the rest of the book, you'll have a greater understanding of its power.

How much do you know about the Moon? Because we see it in the sky so often, it's easy to take it for granted. This section of the book will give you some basic astronomical knowledge about our beautiful Moon.

Lunar facts

First things first. Before we start to discuss the Moon's astrological effects on our lives, we need to understand it from an astronomical point of view.

The origins of the Moon

The Moon is the Earth's only satellite, which means that it's in continual orbit around our planet. Scientists believe that the Moon was formed 4.5 billion years ago, but there are still plenty of theories about how that happened. One of the most compelling modern theories, first postulated in the 1970s, is known as the Big Whack theory, or giant impact hypothesis, to give it its proper (but less arresting) name. This is the theory that the Moon was created when a smaller version of the Earth was involved in a massive collision with another planet, probably two to three times bigger than present-day Mars, producing an incredible amount of flying rock fragments. All this debris eventually coalesced into what we now know as the Moon. This theory still has a long way to go before it can provide clear answers to all the scientific questions connected with the Moon, such as why its core is so small.

The Moon's many craters are thought to be the result of massive meteorite impacts. These craters are known as 'maria', from the Latin word for 'seas', because that's how they looked to early astronomers like Galileo. But don't be fooled – there's no evidence of any water on the Moon. Nor is there evidence of any life on the surface of the Moon, which is hardly surprising when you consider that the Moon doesn't have an atmosphere. Although all its collisions with other space objects, such as asteroids and comets, triggered clouds of gas and therefore an atmosphere, it was only temporary because the Moon's low gravity meant it couldn't hold on to all those gases and they eventually floated away. The Earth, on the other hand, was also involved in many collisions with asteroids but was able to retain the gases that were created, thanks to its high gravitational field.

The dark side of the Moon

We can only see one side of the Moon from our perspective on Earth, and it's always the same side. The other side is known as 'the dark side of the Moon' because it's always hidden from us. It's dark metaphorically too, because we know so little about it. The side that we can see is visible because it reflects the Sun's light back to us (except for the few days leading up to each new moon).

But why do we only ever see one side of the Moon? It's because the Moon completes its orbit of the Earth every 27.3 days (called a sidereal month – something that we'll meet again when we talk about lunar gardening, where it plays a vital role) and, rather neatly, completes a rotation on its axis once every 27.3 Earth days too. Therefore, it only ever shows one face to us. Sometimes, though, that face shows parts of the Moon that at other times would be hidden. Thanks to variations in its orbital speed, the Moon looks like it rocks slightly north–south and wobbles a little east–west – known as its libration. This means a total of 59 per cent of the Moon's surface is illuminated over time, although we can only ever see a maximum of 50 per cent of it at any given moment.

The Moon's orbit

When the Earth and Moon were first formed, they consisted of molten rock. The Earth's much greater mass exerted such a strong gravitational pull on the Moon that it caused a 'bulge' in the side of the Moon facing the Earth. The Moon had to fight against this force, which gradually slowed it down until it stabilized at its current orbital speed.

The Moon's orbit of the Earth is elliptical rather than circular. When the Moon is nearest the Earth (a point known as perigee), it's about 360,000 km (223,700 miles) away; when it's at its furthest point (apogee), the Moon is around 405,000 km (251,700 miles) away. This helps to explain why eclipses of the Sun and Moon are sometimes only partial rather than total – something that becomes particularly important later in this book when we look at the Moon's astrological impact on us.

The lunar cycle

As you now know, the Moon completes its orbit of the Earth once every 27.3 days. You might imagine that this means there's a full moon every 27.3 days too, but that's not the case. A full moon occurs every 29.53 days, and this phase from one full moon to the next (or, indeed, from any specific lunar phase to the next time it occurs) is known as a synodic month. That's because the cycle of new and full Moons is governed by the relationship between the Sun, Earth and the Moon, not just the Moon and the Earth.

The Sun

Before we get on to the subject of new and full moons, we need to talk about the Sun. From our perspective on Earth, the Sun appears to move through the sky as it orbits around our planet, yet the opposite is true: our Earth orbits the Sun. Astrological shorthand refers to the Sun as a planet, but actually it's a star. Being a star means that it rotates in a fixed position in space. Stars don't move but planets do, and indeed the word 'planet' comes from the Greek *planētēs*, meaning 'wanderer'.

Lunar terminology

Sidereal month The 27.3-day period in which the Moon completes its journey through the constellations (such as from Aries to Pisces).

Synodic month The 29.53-day period that elapses between any specific lunar phase and the next time it occurs (such as from one new moon to the next).

Going round in circles

For thousands of years it was widely believed that the Sun and all the known planets revolved around the Earth (a theory known as 'geocentricism'). After all, that was how it looked from our human vantage point, so it had to be true. Then, in 1543,

Polish astronomer Nicolaus Copernicus proposed that the Earth and all the planets revolved in circular orbits around the Sun (a theory known as 'heliocentricism'). Galileo, working in Italy as a renowned astronomer a century later, supported heliocentricism, much to the disgust of the Inquisition, which sentenced him to house arrest for the rest of his life. Finally, in the early 17th century, the German astronomer Johannes Kepler refined Copernicus's ideas by demonstrating that the planets do indeed move in an elliptical orbit around the Sun.

Incidentally, at that time the planets being discussed – other than Earth – were only Mercury, Venus, Mars, Jupiter and Saturn. It took a succession of astronomers over the next 300 years to find the other three. William Herschel discovered Uranus in 1781. Neptune (which Galileo had noticed in 1612 but mistook for one of Jupiter's moons) was first observed by Johann Gottfried Galle in 1846, based on plottings by both Urbain Le Verrier and John Couch Adams, who worked independently on the planet's position and then got into an argument about who had found it first. Finally, in 1930, Clyde Tombaugh found Pluto.

The zodiac

From our perspective on Earth, the Sun, Moon and the eight other planets all follow roughly the same path, known as the ecliptic, through the sky. The ecliptic lies at an angle of 23.5° (the same angle as the Earth's tilt) to the celestial equator – the point at which the Earth's equator would sit if it were extended far into space. In astrology, the ecliptic is divided into twelve sections of 30° each, through which the Sun moves each year. Together, these sections comprise the zodiac – the twelve signs of Aries, Taurus, Gemini, Cancer, Leo, Virgo, Libra, Scorpio, Sagittarius, Capricorn, Aquarius and Pisces. Their names derive from the constellations through which the Sun passes each year, although none of the signs sits neatly within the section bearing its name. This connection with the constellations is why some people talk about a star sign rather than a Sun sign, although Sun sign is the correct term and refers to the section of the zodiac through which the Sun is passing at any one time.

It seems to us on Earth that the Sun, Moon and planets are progressing in a neat course around us, almost as though they're the celestial equivalent of racing cars on a track. However, it's not that simple. Each of them slows down or speeds up at particular points in their journey around the ecliptic, and Pluto has such an erratic path that it sometimes moves within

The dotted line that runs along the blue band of constellations indicates the path of the ecliptic – the path that the Sun appears to take from our perspective on Earth. The celestial equator is an imaginary extension of the Earth's equator.

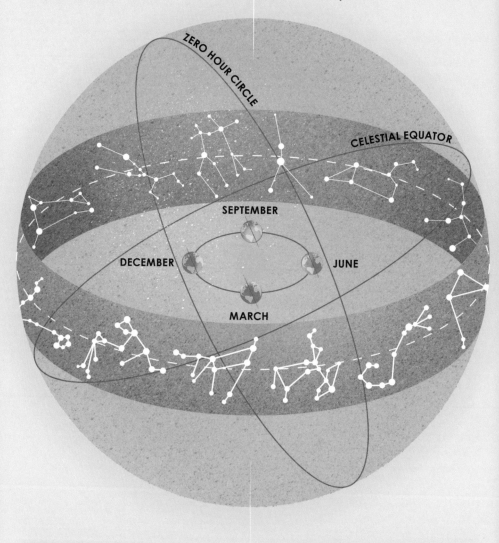

ZERO HOUR CIRCLE

CELESTIAL EQUATOR

SEPTEMBER

DECEMBER

JUNE

MARCH

SUN

EARTH

Neptune's orbit is for a period of twenty years, so during that time it's no longer the outermost planet of the solar system. What's more, each of the planets travels at its own angle to the ecliptic.

The Moon's orbit around the Earth is not a flat plane, and it spends half of each month above the ecliptic (the path of the Sun) and half below it. The points at which the Moon crosses the ecliptic are called the lunar nodes, and they have great astrological significance, as you'll discover in part 2 of this book. The North Node is the point where the Moon rises above the ecliptic, and the South Node is the point where it drops below the ecliptic. The nodal sequence runs backwards, from Pisces to Aries.

The changing Moon

In the astrological system, the Moon is the fastest moving body, and because it completes one journey through the entire zodiac every 29.53 days it enters a new sign roughly every 2.5 days. In other words, it passes through Aries, then through Taurus and so on until it reaches Pisces, before entering Aries again. However, the Moon moves more quickly through some signs than others because of its elliptical orbit. It moves fastest at perigee, when about 45,000 km (28,000 miles) closer to the Earth, than at apogee, when it's at its slowest.

Is Pluto a planet?

Pluto is the smallest of the planets mentioned in this book. It's so small that in 2006, amid much controversy, the International Astronomical Union (IAU) reclassified it as a 'dwarf planet'. In doing this, the IAU also redefined what a planet is. Most astrologers, however, continue to consider that Pluto is a planet – and a very powerful one at that. You don't mess with Pluto!

New moons, full moons and eclipses

If you want to work with the power of the Moon, you don't need a precise understanding of the astronomy involved in the formation of new and full moons, not to mention eclipses. Yet it's a fascinating topic and worth remembering next time you see photos of an eclipse or a full moon. You won't see a new moon, though, because at the point it becomes 'new' (known as its exactitude), it's hidden by the Earth's shadow and therefore completely dark.

When a new moon reaches exactitude, the Sun and Moon occupy the same degree of the zodiac. When a full moon reaches exactitude, the Sun and Moon are 180° apart.

At a new moon, the Moon lies between the Sun and the Earth. At a full moon, the Earth lies between the Sun and the Moon.

Why new and full moons happen

This is where it gets really interesting. We tend to take new and full moons for granted; yet they could be regarded as the result of an extraordinary coincidence. The Moon is approximately 400 times smaller than the Sun, so we're talking about the astronomical equivalent of David and Goliath. However, because the Moon is also approximately 400 times closer to the Earth than the Sun, the Sun and Moon appear pretty much the same size to us on Earth. This situation will eventually change, because the Moon's orbit is getting slightly bigger each year, but that won't affect eclipses for the next several billion years.

Eclipses

At the time of an eclipse, the order of the Sun, Earth and Moon is no different from that of an ordinary new or full moon. What does change is that the three planets are aligned so precisely, and on the same plane, that the Sun's light casts a shadow from either the Earth or the Moon. In a lunar eclipse (see below, also known as an eclipsed full moon), the Moon passes into the shadow cast by the Earth when the Sun is exactly behind it. These eclipses are either total, when the Moon is completely in the Earth's shadow and takes on a reddish glow, or partial, when the Moon passes through the outer part of the Earth's shadow – and it looks as though someone has taken a bite out of the Moon.

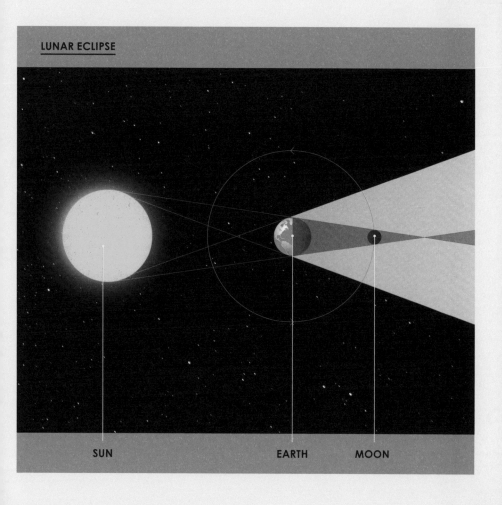

LUNAR ECLIPSE

SUN   EARTH   MOON

In a solar eclipse (see below, also known as an eclipsed new moon), the Moon appears to block out the Sun from our perspective on Earth. There are three types of solar eclipse: total, partial and annular. In the specific locations on Earth affected by a total eclipse, the Sun is completely covered by the shadow of the Moon, and the sky becomes dark. A partial eclipse is exactly that – the Sun is only partially eclipsed by the Moon's shadow. An annular eclipse occurs when the Moon is furthest away from the Earth (at apogee). The Moon therefore looks smaller and doesn't entirely block out the Sun and appears to sit within it, leaving an outer ring of the Sun's light.

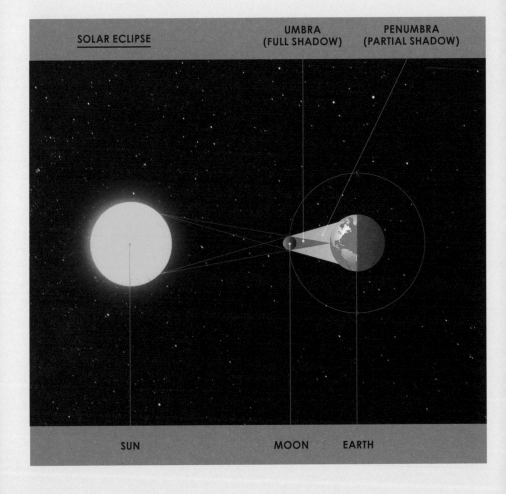

SOLAR ECLIPSE

UMBRA
(FULL SHADOW)

PENUMBRA
(PARTIAL SHADOW)

SUN

MOON

EARTH

Same old, same old

You know what they say about history repeating itself? It certainly does with lunations – the complete cycle of lunar phases in a lunar month. The Greek astronomer Meton, who lived in the 5th century BCE, discovered that the Moon's phases run in a nineteen-year cycle. At the end of every nineteen-year cycle, the lunations recur on the same days of the solar year for the next nineteen years. Please note the crucial word 'solar': this refers to the actual daily motion of the Sun, and not the calendar year that we live by.

Eclipses are part of two cycles – the Metonic cycle and also the Saros cycle. The Saros cycle, which was first discovered by the ancient Babylonians, shows that eclipses belong to a family of other related eclipses – each family lasting for up to two millennia – and that each family produces a solar eclipse (an eclipse of the Sun) approximately every eighteen years, eleven days and eight hours. Each eclipse always occurs 120° of longitude further away than the previous one.

Astro anomalies

In astrology, the Sun and Moon are both referred to as planets. We know full well that the Sun is a star and the Moon is a satellite, but it's easier to refer to them as planets than to have to give their proper description each time. Also, the astrological model most commonly used has the Earth at the centre of the solar system, with the Sun revolving around it. Again, we know that this isn't how things are in space, but it's how they appear to be to us here on Earth.

How the Moon affects us

We can track the Moon's phases by looking up at the sky, but we can also see how it affects our planet day to day simply by walking along the seashore. The ebb and flow of the tide is one of the examples of how the Moon affects our daily lives, thanks to its gravitational pull on the Earth.

The tides

As the Earth and the Moon rotate on their respective axes, the Moon's gravitational pull produces a slight bulge in the part of the Earth it faces at that point. This bulge raises the water levels in that area of the Earth, causing high tides. The Moon's gravitational pull is less strong on the other side of the Earth, where there are low tides. The Earth is spinning all the time, so the bulge moves accordingly, and high tides continually follow the direction in which the Earth rotates.

This lunar effect on the tides is increased at each new and full Moon. The alignment of the Sun and Moon means that the lunar gravitational pull is combined with that of the Sun, resulting in higher or lower tides than usual occurring a short while after a new or full moon. The higher tides are called spring tides, and they get their name from the springing action of the sea rather than because of any seasonal correlation. A spring tide is always followed by a neap tide, during which there's the least difference between high and low tide. A neap tide coincides with the first quarter moon (after a new moon) or the last quarter moon (after a full moon).

Full moon mayhem

Old wives' tales tell us that when the Moon is full people go mad, and the howling of werewolves, ready to attack unsuspecting people out for a moonlit stroll, disturbs the nights. No scientific studies have been conducted on the werewolves, unfortunately, and many scientific studies on the effect of the full moon on our mental health dismiss the idea out of hand. But read on.

Studies have shown that there is indeed a spike in the number of humans who are bitten by animals around the time of a full moon. And the vast majority of those bites come from dogs. As for the link between madness and the full moon, if you consider that the Moon's gravitational pull on the Earth is strong enough to control the oceans' tides, and that each adult human body is up to around 60 per cent water, then you might agree with the theory that the Moon must affect us at a gravitational level too. You might also be interested to know that the staffing levels in hospitals and police stations routinely increase at the time of a full moon. That is because these places are busier than usual, with more hospital admissions and more civil disturbances. Speaking of hospitals, we tend to bleed more easily at the time of a waxing full moon, so it's not a good time to have a surgical procedure if we can possibly avoid it. Also, in one study, cardiac surgery performed during a waning full moon was found to produce a lower mortality rate, with a reduced hospital stay (see pages 134–5).

You can investigate the varying effects of the Moon's phases yourself by listening to the news more carefully whenever there's a new or full moon, and especially during an eclipse. Keep a note of the major incidents that coincide with these lunar phases and you will soon start to see a pattern.

Plant power

One fascinating area of research into the effects of the Moon concerns plants, and it's not just research conducted in a laboratory but empirically in gardens and fields, too. In the 1930s, Lili Kolisko, who was a student of Austrian philosopher and spiritualist Rudolf Steiner, discovered a marked difference in the height of plants raised from seed according to the time when those seeds were sown. Seeds sown two days before a full moon produced much taller plants than those sown at a full moon or two days afterwards. This knowledge became a fundamental part of lunar gardening, which you can read more about in part 5.

THE ASTROLOGICAL MOON

How much do you know about the astrological meaning of the Moon? This section will help you to discover the sign that the Moon occupied when you were born and how that influences your habits and all the things in life that feel familiar to you. It will also reveal how well your Sun and Moon signs get along with each other, and what they say about you.

You probably already know quite a lot about your Sun sign – sometimes called your star sign – but you may not know much at all about your Moon sign. Yet it's one of the most important parts of your natal chart!

2

What the Moon represents

In astrology, every planet in the solar system has a specific sphere of influence and meaning. The Moon is no different, and because it's the Earth's satellite, and has such a strong relationship with the Sun, it's a very important part of the birth chart. Here are some of the areas that the Moon represents and influences.

Familiarity breeds content

The sign that your Moon occupied when you were born describes everything that you find familiar. These are the areas of life that you return to, whether mentally, emotionally or physically, whenever you're in need of comfort.

The Moon also describes your habits and instincts. Your habits are just that – actions that have become second nature and a part of your life. Your instincts are the knee-jerk, gut reactions that happen almost unconsciously. The Moon isn't interested in logic and reason, so these instinctive responses are based on your immediate emotions when confronted by particular situations. Sometimes, as we get older, we realize that some of these responses – such as panic or a desire for escape – may not be helpful for us and we train ourselves to take note of them but not necessarily to act on them. We might, for instance, learn deep-breathing techniques so we can calm down, or remind ourselves that we need to stay present in order to find effective ways to deal with what's happening.

Home sweet home

One of the Moon's most significant areas of rulership is the home and family. Your Moon sign tells you what family and home mean to you, and this is very personal. It can be extremely subjective, so someone with the Moon in Cancer, whose world revolves around their domestic life, might be astonished that their friend with the Moon in Sagittarius treats their home more like a hotel, possibly even only being there when they don't have anything better to do.

The Moon also describes the sort of family you were born into and how you experienced it. This explains why, if you have siblings, they may not have the same Moon sign as you and might not see your family in the same way, either. Did family life involve strict rules about what you could and couldn't do (Moon in Taurus or Capricorn) or was it easy-going and relaxed (Moon in Gemini or Sagittarius)? Did the death of an important member of the family, up to a couple of years before you were born, mean that your family's long-standing grief mingled with joy at your arrival (something that happens for a surprising number of people born with the Moon in Scorpio)?

Food

The Moon has a nurturing influence, so it rules food too. Not only can it describe the food you like to eat but also how it affects you emotionally. You might regard food as your primary source of health and wellbeing, so are very strict about what you eat (Moon in Virgo) or you might adore the sensual pleasure of eating your favourite foods, even if they aren't all that good for you (Moon in Libra).

Health

The Moon also represents various parts of the body, including the breasts, stomach and bodily fluids. However, medical astrology is a complex topic and requires not only astrological but medical knowledge if it's to be practised properly. Therefore, it's beyond the scope of this book.

Delving deeper

The following pages will show you how to discover your own Moon sign and also give you a good introduction to that sign. If you want to know more, such as discovering the aspects (see page 33) that your Moon makes to other planets in your chart and how these describe you and your past, you can consult a professional astrologer who will help you to unpick all these threads and make sense of them.

The Moon-sign finder

If you already know the sign of your Moon when you were born, perhaps because you've consulted an astrologer or looked up your birth chart online, you don't need to read about this because you've already got the vital information. However, if you're wondering which sign the Moon occupied when you were born, you're about to find out.

CHART 1

YEAR						
1920	1939	1958	1977	1996	2015	
1921	1940	1959	1978	1997	2016	
1922	1941	1960	1979	1998	2017	
1923	1942	1961	1980	1999	2018	
1924	1943	1962	1981	2000	2019	
1925	1944	1963	1982	2001	2020	
1926	1945	1964	1983	2002	2021	
1927	1946	1965	1984	2003	2022	
1928	1947	1966	1985	2004	2023	
1929	1948	1967	1986	2005	2024	
1930	1949	1968	1987	2006	2025	
1931	1950	1969	1988	2007	2026	
1932	1951	1970	1989	2008	2027	
1933	1952	1971	1990	2009	2028	
1934	1953	1972	1991	2010	2029	
1935	1954	1973	1992	2011	2030	
1936	1955	1974	1993	2012	2031	
1937	1956	1975	1994	2013	2032	
1938	1957	1976	1995	2014	2033	

The charts on this and the following pages will help you to not only discover your own Moon sign but also learn the position of the Moon on all sorts of other occasions. Want to know where the Moon was when you first met your partner or when you got married? These charts will tell you. Are you wondering about your child's Moon sign, or maybe your pet's? Once again, these charts will give you the information you need.

But they don't only look at the past. They can give you an insight into the future, too, by revealing the sign that will be occupied by the Moon on any given day up to the end of 2033.

The method is exactly the same whether you're looking back into the past or ahead into the future. The following pages will explain what to do.

MOON SIGNS ON THE FIRST DAY OF EACH MONTH

JAN	FEB	MAR	APR	MAY	JUN	JUL	AUG	SEP	OCT	NOV	DEC
ARI	CAN	CAN	VIR	LIB	SAG	CAP	AQU	ARI	VIR	SCO	SAG
LIB	SCO	SAG	CAP	AQU	ARI	TAU	CAN	LEO	AQU	ARI	TAU
AQU	ARI	ARI	GEM	CAN	LEO	VIR	SCO	CAP	GEM	LEO	VIR
GEM	LEO	LEO	LIB	SCO	CAP	AQU	ARI	TAU	SCO	SAG	CAP
SCO	SAG	CAP	AQU	ARI	TAU	GEM	LEO	LIB	PISC	TAU	GEM
PISC	TAU	TAU	CAN	LEO	LIB	SCO	SAG	AQU	LEO	VIR	LIB
LEO	VIR	LIB	SCO	SAG	AQU	PISC	TAU	CAN	SAG	AQU	PISC
SAG	CAP	AQU	PISC	TAU	GEM	LEO	VIR	SCO	ARI	GEM	CAN
ARI	GEM	GEM	LEO	VIR	SCO	SAG	AQU	PISC	VIR	LIB	SAG
VIR	SCO	SCO	CAP	AQU	PISC	TAU	GEM	LEO	CAP	PISC	ARI
CAP	PISC	PISC	TAU	GEM	LEO	VIR	SCO	SAG	GEM	CAN	LEO
TAU	CAN	CAN	VIR	LIB	SAG	CAP	PISC	ARI	LIB	SAG	CAP
LIB	SAG	SAG	AQU	PISC	TAU	GEM	CAN	VIR	LIB	SAG	CAP
PISC	ARI	TAU	GEM	CAN	VIR	LIB	SAG	CAP	AQU	ARI	TAU
CAN	VIR	VIR	LIB	SAG	CAP	PISC	ARI	GEM	CAN	VIR	LIB
SCO	CAP	CAP	PISC	ARI	GEM	CAN	VIR	SCO	SAG	CAP	AQU
ARI	TAU	GEM	LEO	VIR	LIB	SCO	CAP	PISC	ARI	TAU	CAN
LEO	LIB	LIB	SAG	CAP	PISC	ARI	TAU	CAN	LEO	LIB	SCO
CAP	AQU	PISC	ARI	TAU	CAN	LEO	LIB	SCO	CAP	AQU	ARI

1 Go to chart 1 • YEARS AND MONTHS

Locate the year you want – whether that's a birth year or the year of a particular event – in the column on pages 26. When you've found it, follow that horizontal line to the chart showing the Moon signs for the first day of each month. Make sure you stay on the same line. Write down the sign that you find.

2 Go to chart 2 • DAYS OF THE MONTH

Find the day of the month for the date in question. Look at the vertical column immediately below it to discover the number of signs you must add from the first day of that month. Write this down too.

CHART 2

									DAY																					
1	2	3	4	5	6	7	8	9	10	11	12	13	14	15	16	17	18	19	20	21	22	23	24	25	26	27	28	29	30	31
0	1	1	1	2	2	3	3	4	4	5	5	5	6	6	7	7	8	8	9	9	10	10	10	11	11	12	12	1	1	2

ADD (NUMBER OF SIGNS)

3 Go to chart 3 • ZODIAC WHEEL

Find the sign that you wrote down in step 1. Working clockwise from this sign, count forwards the number of signs that you were given in step 2. The resulting zodiac sign is the sign for the day and year that you have looked up.

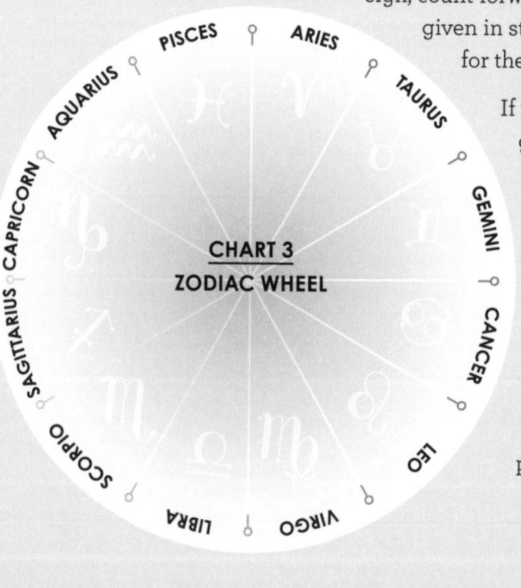

If you want to find the day when the Moon is going to be in the most favourable sign for a particular task or action, you can locate the correct year and month as before in chart 1, and then count around chart 3 until you find the sign you're looking for. Write down the number of signs that you've counted, and then consult chart 2 to find this number in the 'add' column. This will tell you the days of the month when the Moon is in that particular sign.

CHART 3
ZODIAC WHEEL

PISCES • ARIES • TAURUS • GEMINI • CANCER • LEO • VIRGO • LIBRA • SCORPIO • SAGITTARIUS • CAPRICORN • AQUARIUS

Example for a favourable day in the future

This is an example of what you do when you're looking ahead. Let's say that you want to throw a big birthday party in early July 2020, and you've decided that it has got to be when the Moon is in Leo. As before, you look at chart 1 to find the relevant year. Then you follow that horizontal line until you reach July. This tells you that the Moon will be in Scorpio on the first day of July. Write this down! Now you turn to chart 3 and find Scorpio. Count round the zodiac wheel until you reach Leo and take note of this number, which is nine. (Remember that you start counting from the next sign, which in this case is Sagittarius, not from Scorpio itself.) Now look for nine signs in chart 2 to find the dates in July 2020 when the Moon will be in Leo. These are the 20th and 21st.

Checking the location of your birth or a future event The Moon-sign finder charts relate to Greenwich Mean Time (GMT) or Universal Time (UT) – or Coordinated Universal Time (UTC) as it's now also called. That's because the Earth is so large that it's divided up into twenty-four vertical segments of different time zones, starting at 0° longitude at the Greenwich meridian in London, UK. Some parts of the world keep the same time as GMT because they have the same longitude, but the vast majority have their own time zone that runs either ahead or behind GMT.

In astrology, all times have to be converted back to GMT before a chart can be calculated. In the past, before the days of computers, this conversion was done by hand and could be a complicated and time-consuming business, but thankfully now there are computer programs that do it at the click of a mouse. So, if you weren't born in the UK or in its time zone, you can refer to the Resources section on page 173 to find some of the websites that will calculate your birth chart based on the time and location of your birth.

Example for a date of birth

Let's say you were born on 8 May 1988. If you look at chart 1 along the horizontal line for 1988, you can see that the Moon was in Libra on the first day of May. If you turn to chart 2, you can see that you have to add three signs to Libra to discover your Moon sign. If you go to chart 3 and count three signs on from Libra, you arrive at Capricorn. Therefore, you were born with the Sun in Taurus and the Moon in Capricorn.

Natal moon in Aries

If you were born with an Aries moon, here's some essential information to help you understand yourself. You can also use this to understand someone you know with the Moon in Aries. But the Moon doesn't work in isolation – the facing page tells you how your Moon fits with your Sun sign. You can also use this combination to discover how your Moon gets on with other Sun signs.

ELEMENT: **Fire**

MODE: **cardinal**

KEYWORDS: **pioneering, assertive**

Whatever you want in life, you want it now! After all, Aries is the first sign of the zodiac, so the Moon here confers a 'me first!' attitude. Your instinct is to get on with life. You can't bear to be kept hanging about, and you soon get impatient if you have to wait too long for something. This means that you're often in a hurry, which is when the problems can start. The Moon in Aries gives you the instinctive tendency to rush into a new idea or project with a huge burst of enthusiasm and idealism. Unfortunately, you may be in such a hurry to get started that you overlook some important considerations, such as whether the idea is feasible or whether you'll still be interested in it next week. As a result, you may quickly get bored, leaving a trail of unfinished projects in your wake.

When it comes to tuning into other people's feelings, you find it difficult to put yourself in their shoes. You assume that they feel the same way as you do about things and are surprised or even offended if you discover that they don't.

Where you excel is in following your own destiny. Aries as a sign wants to be a pioneer and to take the lead, so when you have the Moon here you instinctively take charge, whether it's of other people or a situation. You don't see this as bossy behaviour – you simply feel the need to make things happen quickly. Also, you have a strong need for independence and to be your unique self, so you hate the thought of trailing along behind other people or doing what they tell you.

Your instinct for urgent action means you really come into your own when faced with a problem or emergency. While other moon signs are fussing or going into a panic, you automatically take charge. Your Aries courage gives you the ability to do whatever is necessary. You will stand up for the underdog if you think they need your help, and champion anyone who could do with some of your inspirational encouragement.

SUN IN ARIES, MOON IN ARIES
Independent; assertive; dynamic; impatient; eager for challenges; self-centred; energetic

SUN IN TAURUS, MOON IN ARIES
Forceful; powers of endurance; stubborn; need for security; practicality versus idealism

SUN IN GEMINI, MOON IN ARIES
Lively; restless; sociable; enterprising; quick-witted; great at generating ideas

SUN IN CANCER, MOON IN ARIES
Purposeful; determined; moody; defensive; affectionate; supportive; warm-hearted

SUN IN LEO, MOON IN ARIES
Enthusiastic; joie de vivre; energetic; creative; dramatic; egotistic; courageous; subjective

SUN IN VIRGO, MOON IN ARIES
Clever; analytical; an eye for detail; nervy; restless; workaholic; sharp-tongued; critical

SUN IN LIBRA, MOON IN ARIES
Affectionate; caring; gains self-awareness through others; diplomatic; strong sense of justice

SUN IN SCORPIO, MOON IN ARIES
Powerful; determined; driven; argumentative; intense; volatile; tempestuous; magnetic

SUN IN SAGITTARIUS, MOON IN ARIES
Vibrant; optimistic; curious; a free spirit; honest; tactless; fiery temper; impractical; generous

SUN IN CAPRICORN, MOON IN ARIES
Hard-working; motivated; competitive; focused; stamina; serious; materialistic; blunt

SUN IN AQUARIUS, MOON IN ARIES
Flair; inventive; independent; hates being given orders; courageous; self-involved

SUN IN PISCES, MOON IN ARIES
Sensitive; romantic; idealistic; a dreamer; huffy; artistic; needs a direction in life

Natal moon in Taurus

If you were born with a Taurus moon, here's some essential information to help you understand yourself. You can also use this to understand someone you know with the Moon in Taurus. But the Moon doesn't work in isolation – the facing page tells you how your Moon fits with your Sun sign. You can also use this combination to discover how your Moon gets on with other Sun signs.

ELEMENT: **Earth**

MODE: **fixed**

KEYWORDS: **steady, stable**

People know where they are with you. You're calm, steady and dependable. If you say you're going to do something, you do it, because you hate the thought of letting anyone down. Performing tasks in a hurry makes you feel rushed because you prefer to take your time and work at a steady pace rather than dash around in a panic. This helps to keep you calm and ensures that you're productive and practical. When faced with a problem, you're persistent and determined. However, this can sometimes lead to stubbornness, and possibly even the conviction that hell will freeze over before you alter your mind about something.

Change – especially if it's imposed on you – feels like such a monumental challenge and threat because you have a deep, instinctive need for physical and emotional security. You like things to stay as they are, even if you aren't entirely happy with them. This means that being stuck in a rut may feel like a better option than having to disrupt the status quo, with all the risks that may involve.

Your liking for stability affects your relationships too, making you loyal, loving and steadfast. You are patient and placid, and you have to be really provoked before you lose your temper. The sign of Taurus is associated with possessions and material things, and sometimes the Moon here can suggest a possessive attitude to loved ones, with a reluctance to let them go their own way.

SUN IN ARIES, MOON IN TAURUS
Dynamic; action backed up by
determination; Aries impatience at odds
with Taurean steadiness

SUN IN TAURUS, MOON IN TAURUS
Down-to-earth; steady; resistant to
change; obstinate; practical; sensual;
possessive

SUN IN GEMINI, MOON IN TAURUS
Witty; entertaining; interested in others;
Gemini quickness tempered by Taurean
slowness

SUN IN CANCER, MOON IN TAURUS
Kind; reassuring; affectionate;
traditional; family-minded; reluctant to
step outside comfort zone

SUN IN LEO, MOON IN TAURUS
Loyal; artistic; loving; obstinate; dogged;
persistent; sensuous; luxury-loving;
reliable

SUN IN VIRGO, MOON IN TAURUS
Grounded; practical; sensible;
methodical; hard-working; resolute;
nature-loving; hates change

SUN IN LIBRA, MOON IN TAURUS
Hedonistic; creative; artistic flair and
appreciation; stylish; affectionate;
romantic; sentimental

SUN IN SCORPIO, MOON IN TAURUS
Powerful; emotional intensity; prone to
possessiveness; financial acumen;
dogmatic; steadfast

**SUN IN SAGITTARIUS, MOON IN
TAURUS**
Sagittarian wanderlust clashes with
Taurean stability; enthusiastic;
supportive; musical

**SUN IN CAPRICORN, MOON IN
TAURUS**
Stable; common sense; pragmatic;
motivated; earthy; strong personality;
dependable

SUN IN AQUARIUS, MOON IN TAURUS
Aquarian independence versus Taurean
need for security; determined;
intransigent; loyal

SUN IN PISCES, MOON IN TAURUS
Kind; considerate; sensitive; warm;
charming; artistic; musical; appreciative;
moody

Natal moon in Gemini

If you were born with a Gemini moon, here's some essential information to help you understand yourself. You can also use this to understand someone you know with the Moon in Gemini. But the Moon doesn't work in isolation – the facing page tells you how your Moon fits with your Sun sign. You can also use this combination to discover how your Moon gets on with other Sun signs.

ELEMENT: **Air**

MODE: **mutable**

KEYWORDS: **quick, changeable**

The sign of Gemini is often compared to a butterfly because of a tendency to flit from one thing to another. You're no exception, with an innate versatility and restlessness, so your natural instinct is to switch from one activity to another as the fancy takes you. This stops you getting stale and stimulates your very clever brain. You may even be able to do two or more things at once without even realizing it, such as watching TV while reading a book. It's an ability that comes naturally to you, as is being dextrous with your hands. You might even be ambidextrous. Whenever you get nervous, you fidget, tap your feet or pace the room, because keeping on the move helps you to calm down. Enforced idleness doesn't suit you at all. Your phone or tablet goes everywhere with you, because you never know when you'll need to ring someone or take an interesting photo.

Conversations and gossip feed you both emotionally and intellectually. What's more, you're highly entertaining, with a mischievous sense of fun, ready wit, playful nature and remarkable ability to move seamlessly from a serious conversation to jokey wordplay. Nevertheless, sometimes you may have to remind yourself of the importance of listening, rather than holding the floor. What few people realize is that you're always looking for a soul mate – someone who feels like your twin. And what you may not realize is that you won't find it in other people – because it resides in you.

SUN IN ARIES, MOON IN GEMINI
Busy; lively; chatty; Aries energy drives
Gemini ideas; needs variety and plenty
of outside interests

SUN IN TAURUS, MOON IN GEMINI
Taurean stability is livened up by
Gemini flexibility; warm and friendly;
emotions can be erratic

SUN IN GEMINI, MOON IN GEMINI
Quicksilver moods; happier with ideas
than emotions; witty; inquisitive; easily
bored; chatty

SUN IN CANCER, MOON IN GEMINI
Lively conversation; creative interests;
clash between Cancerian emotion and
Gemini intellect

SUN IN LEO, MOON IN GEMINI
Artistic; sociable; entertaining;
commanding personality; clever ideas
coupled with determination

SUN IN VIRGO, MOON IN GEMINI
Bright personality; clever and agile
mind; nervous energy; analytical;
focuses on facts not feelings

SUN IN LIBRA, MOON IN GEMINI
Charming; diplomatic; engaging; clever
conversation; uncomfortable with
powerful emotions

SUN IN SCORPIO, MOON IN GEMINI
Ability to put deep feelings into words;
curiosity; Scorpio intensity clashes with
Gemini lightness

**SUN IN SAGITTARIUS, MOON IN
GEMINI**
Intellectual; love of books; fascinated by
the world; restless; yearns for travel and
adventure

**SUN IN CAPRICORN, MOON IN
GEMINI**
Serious and flippant by turns; engaging
sense of humour; reliance on the rational
side of life

SUN IN AQUARIUS, MOON IN GEMINI
Good friend; clever and agile mind;
intellectual; focuses on ideas to the
detriment of emotions

SUN IN PISCES, MOON IN GEMINI
Intuitive; sensitive; artistic; flexible;
escapist tendencies when confronted by
difficult situations

Natal moon in Cancer

If you were born with a Cancerian moon, here's some essential information to help you understand yourself. You can also use this to understand someone you know with the Moon in Cancer. But the Moon doesn't work in isolation – the facing page tells you how your Moon fits with your Sun sign. You can also use this combination to discover how your Moon gets on with other Sun signs.

ELEMENT: **Water**

MODE: **cardinal**

KEYWORDS: **emotional security, tenacious**

Cancer is the sign ruled by the Moon, so this is a very strong placing. Regardless of your gender, you brim with maternal instincts. You're protective, loving and kind towards the people you care about, with a tendency to feed them up at every opportunity. It's one of your ways of showing affection. You have an overwhelming need for emotional security, and once you find it – whether in a person, place or possession – you'll cling to it as tightly as possible. This can sometimes mean that you hold on to a relationship, home or object long after you should have let it go. It feels comfortingly familiar, even if it's holding you back or no longer serves you – and severing the ties can be extremely painful.

You adore having your favourite people around you and can feel upset or even offended when other commitments take them away from you. Cancer is the sign of the family, so being part of a family group is essential to your happiness. If, for some reason, you can't have that with the family you were born into, you'll create a tightknit, secure and affectionate group of friends who feel like family.

Your emotions influence every aspect of your life. You can't switch them off and pretend they don't exist, so you tend to wear your heart on your sleeve. It's obvious when you're happy, and there's also no mistaking when you're not, because you become moody, defensive and huffy.

SUN IN ARIES, MOON IN CANCER
Ambitious; go-getting; defensive; emotionally sensitive; independent streak yet periodically needy

SUN IN TAURUS, MOON IN CANCER
Needs emotional and physical security, close-knit family and friends; conservative; practical

SUN IN GEMINI, MOON IN CANCER
Born collector of things and people; affectionate and warm; sociable; considerate; moody

SUN IN CANCER, MOON IN CANCER
Warm; supportive of others; easily swayed by emotions; family-orientated; emotionally needy

SUN IN LEO, MOON IN CANCER
Expansive; affectionate; creative; generous; Leo enthusiasm tempered by Cancerian caution

SUN IN VIRGO, MOON IN CANCER
Industrious; reliable; businesslike; house-proud; Virgoan reserve warmed by Cancerian emotion

SUN IN LIBRA, MOON IN CANCER
Ambition and drive; sociable; charming; considerate; indecisive; gift for friendship; sentimental

SUN IN SCORPIO, MOON IN CANCER
Deep emotions, but can be protective of them; intuitive; sensitive; moody; a devoted partner

SUN IN SAGITTARIUS, MOON IN CANCER
Vivid enthusiasms; love of history; fascinated by people; optimism can cause disappointment

SUN IN CAPRICORN, MOON IN CANCER
Motivated; respect for tradition and doing things properly; determined; sense of humour

SUN IN AQUARIUS, MOON IN CANCER
Aquarian rationality warmed by Cancerian compassion; kind; considerate; humanitarian

SUN IN PISCES, MOON IN CANCER
Highly emotional; easily swayed by others; deep need for familiarity; instinctive and intuitive

Natal moon in Leo

If you were born with a Leo moon, here's some essential information to help you understand yourself. You can also use this to understand someone you know with the Moon in Leo. But the Moon doesn't work in isolation – the facing page tells you how your Moon fits with your Sun sign. You can also use this combination to discover how your Moon gets on with other Sun signs.

ELEMENT: **Fire**

MODE: **fixed**

KEYWORDS: **dignified, creative**

Having the Moon in Leo gives you a tremendous need for creative self-expression. That might mean getting involved in artistic activities, such as painting or making your own clothes, or maybe your Leo love of drama inspires you to act or sing. After all, Leo is a sign that loves being centre stage. Sometimes the whole of your life can feel like a drama, with you playing the starring role. This is especially likely if you were brought up to believe that you always have to put a brave face on things and keep smiling, even when you feel unhappy or depressed. After all, the show must go on. If you feel you can't reveal your true turmoil because that would lack dignity, you may find that you tend to create a scene about something minor instead. Sometimes you might feel much better if you could admit that you're going through a tough time and need to look after yourself.

This is an extremely loving and affectionate sign, making you warm, demonstrative and generous. You adore surrounding yourself with the people you love, and you may have an especially soft spot for children. Leo is the sign ruled by the Sun, the centre of our solar system, and you also enjoy being at the centre of your own universe, with a love of the limelight. You revel in other people's compliments and appreciation and are generous in being equally complimentary yourself. However, an element of competition can occasionally creep into your relationships if you sense that someone might steal your thunder and put you in the shade.

SUN IN ARIES, MOON IN LEO
Enthusiastic; energetic; warm and loving; idealistic; can be bossy and demanding

SUN IN TAURUS, MOON IN LEO
Strong-willed; loyal; reliable; proud; affectionate; supportive; strong sense of self-esteem

SUN IN GEMINI, MOON IN LEO
Amusing; quick-witted; creative; entertaining companion; big personality

SUN IN CANCER, MOON IN LEO
Loving; openly affectionate; needs to belong; protective of loved ones; loyal; sentimental

SUN IN LEO, MOON IN LEO
Expansive; demonstrative; theatrical; artistic; demanding; must consider the needs of others

SUN IN VIRGO, MOON IN LEO
Precise; ordered; Virgo reserve warmed by Leo enthusiasm; dignified; creative

SUN IN LIBRA, MOON IN LEO
Very focused on relationships; can be in love with love; artistic talents; generous; affectionate

SUN IN SCORPIO, MOON IN LEO
Steadfast; dogmatic; charismatic; determined; loyal; dislikes contradiction

SUN IN SAGITTARIUS, MOON IN LEO
Expansive; optimistic; romantic and idealistic; adventurous; impatient

SUN IN CAPRICORN, MOON IN LEO
Powerful motivation and ambition; wants to be taken seriously; proud; supportive of loved ones

SUN IN AQUARIUS, MOON IN LEO
Open-hearted and humanitarian; proud to be an individual; dazzling personality; controlling

SUN IN PISCES, MOON IN LEO
Tender-hearted and kind; highly creative; Pisces sensitivity strengthened by Leo pride

Natal moon in Virgo

If you were born with a Virgo moon, here's some essential information to help you understand yourself. You can also use this to understand someone you know with the Moon in Virgo. But the Moon doesn't work in isolation – the facing page tells you how your Moon fits with your Sun sign. You can also use this combination to discover how your Moon gets on with other Sun signs.

ELEMENT: **Earth**

MODE: **mutable**

KEYWORDS: **perfectionist, service**

Taking life gently isn't really an option for you. You believe in doing things properly and not cutting corners; so, you are quite prepared to work round the clock when necessary. This makes you ultra-reliable and efficient – someone that others can depend on. Failing to meet your own high standards triggers two of your bugbears – self-criticism and the anxiety that so often dogs you. You always think that you could do better, and if you get really wound up you tend to project that on to others, nagging them that they ought to pull their socks up, too.

Virgo is a highly analytical sign, so your mind can get caught up in an endless loop of overthinking, worrying and nervous tension, all of which leave you drained and tense. Despite this, you love being busy, so you're always on the go, with a real need to be helpful to others. Making sure that someone is OK is your way of showing that you care. Overt displays of love and affection can make you feel uncomfortable, so you're much happier with something more modest. This doesn't mean that you have no feelings; it simply means you can struggle to express them. You should, therefore, find positive outlets for all your emotions, otherwise they have a habit of turning inwards and triggering physical ailments or illnesses. Finding ways to truly relax will do you good, too.

SUN IN ARIES, MOON IN VIRGO
A real live wire; Aries initiative backed up by Virgo precision; non-stop activity comes at a price

SUN IN TAURUS, MOON IN VIRGO
Practical; realistic; measured; focuses on material security; common sense; supportive

SUN IN GEMINI, MOON IN VIRGO
Buzzy; rapid thought processes; nervous energy needs positive outlets; emotionally reserved

SUN IN CANCER, MOON IN VIRGO
Emphasis on a well-run home life; charming and considerate; tendency to fret over trifles

SUN IN LEO, MOON IN VIRGO
Leo sense of drama curbed by Virgo modesty; precise and methodical creative skills; sense of humour

SUN IN VIRGO, MOON IN VIRGO
Self-imposed high standards; sharp intellect and wit; self-critical; analytical and clever

SUN IN LIBRA, MOON IN VIRGO
Diplomatic and tactful; Libran indecision tempered by Virgoan efficiency; kind and caring; intelligent

SUN IN SCORPIO, MOON IN VIRGO
Highly motivated to succeed; strong will; skilled with words; honest but can be critical

SUN IN SAGITTARIUS, MOON IN VIRGO
Fascinated by the world; enquiring mind; straightforward but can be blunt; nervy

SUN IN CAPRICORN, MOON IN VIRGO
Industrious and eager to succeed; strong moral compass; raunchy and sexy

SUN IN AQUARIUS, MOON IN VIRGO
Can live in the mind; emphasis on the intellect and rationality; cool emotions; kind and loyal

SUN IN PISCES, MOON IN VIRGO
Pisces idealism grounded by Virgo common sense; creative gifts; kind, considerate and caring

Natal moon in Libra

If you were born with a Libra moon, here's some essential information to help you understand yourself. You can also use this to understand someone you know with the Moon in Libra. But the Moon doesn't work in isolation – the facing page tells you how your Moon fits with your Sun sign. You can also use this combination to discover how your Moon gets on with other Sun signs.

ELEMENT: **Air**

MODE: **cardinal**

KEYWORDS: **balance, fairness**

The scales symbolize Libra – they show your need for balance at all times. Although your moods may swing in one direction and then another, you strive for a happy medium and for equilibrium. Dealing successfully with other people is one of your greatest skills, thanks to your innate courtesy, charm and diplomacy. You believe in being polite whenever possible and will go out of your way to pacify people, because you'd much rather have harmony than hostility. In fact, you hate being faced by too much aggression, and even ordinary domestic bickering can get you down if it goes on for too long.

You excel at relationships, which is just as well because, generally speaking, you feel much happier when you're with others than when you're by yourself. In extreme cases you may even cling to a relationship long after it should have ended simply because you hate the prospect of being solo again.

Being a people-pleaser means you sometimes put your own needs to one side in order to keep the peace, because you don't want to risk a confrontation by voicing your own opinion and then find that other people don't agree with it. If you do this too often you can feel resentful and may even end up having the row that you were so keen to avert. Another factor is your ability to see at least two sides to every story, which gives you your highly regarded sense of fair play but can also lead to indecision. How can you make up your mind when you're aware of the pros and cons of every possible action?

SUN IN ARIES, MOON IN LIBRA
Affectionate; considerate; enjoyment of other people; idealistic

SUN IN TAURUS, MOON IN LIBRA
Sensual; hedonistic; strong creative and artistic streak; romantic; a gourmet

SUN IN GEMINI, MOON IN LIBRA
Intelligent; skilled communicator; clever sense of humour; wary of emotional displays

SUN IN CANCER, MOON IN LIBRA
Motivated; needs a close circle of friends and family; struggles to end relationships

SUN IN LEO, MOON IN LIBRA
Only the best will do; extravagant; creative; emotionally warm; adores love and romance

SUN IN VIRGO, MOON IN LIBRA
High standards; painstaking; wants to make a good impression; can be reserved emotionally

SUN IN LIBRA, MOON IN LIBRA
Charismatic; courteous; wants to win the affection of others; indecisive; needs other people

SUN IN SCORPIO, MOON IN LIBRA
Emotional intensity expressed with charm; controlled behaviour; sociable but needs privacy

SUN IN SAGITTARIUS, MOON IN LIBRA
Enterprising; intellectual interests; fascinated by other people; friendly and outgoing

SUN IN CAPRICORN, MOON IN LIBRA
Capricorn reserve warmed by Libran charm; hard-working; strong moral code

SUN IN AQUARIUS, MOON IN LIBRA
Clever; cool emotionally, but a faithful friend; naive streak can lead to disappointments

SUN IN PISCES, MOON IN LIBRA
Highly considerate; a born romantic; idealistic and easily hurt; artistic and musical

Natal moon in Scorpio

If you were born with a Scorpio moon, here's some essential information to help you understand yourself. You can also use this to understand someone you know with the Moon in Scorpio. But the Moon doesn't work in isolation – the facing page tells you how your Moon fits with your Sun sign. You can also use this combination to discover how your Moon gets on with other Sun signs.

ELEMENT: **Water**

MODE: **fixed**

KEYWORDS: **intense, controlled**

This is the most complex placing of all for the Moon, because it's the planet of emotion and the unconscious in the sign of deep emotional intensity. Whatever you choose to do in life, you'll want to do it with great conviction and commitment, really pouring your heart and soul into it. Just going through the motions isn't for you, and you feel dissatisfied with yourself whenever you find yourself doing it. You have tremendous reserves of willpower, resilience and self-control, so you can endure difficulties and tribulations that would daunt other Moon signs, but which add to your experience of the ways of the world. It's quite likely that this began at an early age, when life presented you with a series of emotional hurdles to negotiate. As a result of these experiences you may find it hard to trust people, or you may feel suspicious of their motives, even when you know them really well. Is this paranoia or simply first-hand knowledge of what people are capable of?

When it comes to dealing with difficult emotions, you'll either bottle them up or be very outspoken about them – it's all or nothing with you! It's important for you to find a constructive outlet for these turbulent feelings, even though you may never be able to explore them fully because of their complexity and depth. You may also realize that you need to have more faith in others, and that if you want to change the status quo you can only change yourself, not them.

SUN IN ARIES, MOON IN SCORPIO
Determined; dynamic; powerful
personality; argumentative; kind;
protective

SUN IN TAURUS, MOON IN SCORPIO
Strong-willed; stubborn; controlling;
possessive; loving; supportive; loyal;
sensual

SUN IN GEMINI, MOON IN SCORPIO
Quick-witted; lively imagination; sharp
tongue; chatty; ability to express
profound emotions

SUN IN CANCER, MOON IN SCORPIO
Emotional; intuitive; sensitive; moody;
defensive; deep interest in other people

SUN IN LEO, MOON IN SCORPIO
Proud; dignified; Leo openness contrasts
with Scorpio secrecy; steadfast friend
and lover

SUN IN VIRGO, MOON IN SCORPIO
Clever way with words; witty; sarcastic;
industrious; indefatigable; perceptive

SUN IN LIBRA, MOON IN SCORPIO
Strong sense of justice; emotionally cool
but loves intensely; level-headed

SUN IN SCORPIO, MOON IN SCORPIO
Powerful and intense; emotions are kept
under tight control; need for privacy;
very loyal

**SUN IN SAGITTARIUS, MOON IN
SCORPIO**
Great interest in knowing what makes
people tick; intelligent and inquisitive;
trustworthy friend

**SUN IN CAPRICORN, MOON IN
SCORPIO**
Sensible; plenty of common sense;
businesslike; controlled but very sincere
emotions

**SUN IN AQUARIUS, MOON IN
SCORPIO**
Powerful opinions; obstinate; strong-
willed; loyal and supportive; loving but
undemonstrative

SUN IN PISCES, MOON IN SCORPIO
Keen instincts and intuition; artistic
abilities; can have profound dreams;
very emotional

Natal moon in Sagittarius

If you were born with a Sagittarius moon, here's some essential information to help you understand yourself. You can also use this to understand someone you know with the Moon in Sagittarius. But the Moon doesn't work in isolation – the facing page tells you how your Moon fits with your Sun sign. You can also use this combination to discover how your Moon gets on with other Sun signs.

ELEMENT: **Fire**

MODE: **mutable**

KEYWORDS: **exploration, optimism**

The call of the open road and the thought of its endless possibilities really appeal to you. You may never act on it, but you love the thought of taking off somewhere so you can be free to do what you like. You may even dream of getting on a plane with just your phone, passport and a credit card, and heading off for who knows where. But it's not only physical travel that calls to you, because you have a deep-seated need to take off on mental journeys too. Sagittarius is the sign of knowledge, so you're on a lifelong course of learning and truth, whether that means college or university, or simply soaking up a wealth of experience over the years. All sorts of ideas appeal to you, but you're particularly drawn to history, international concerns and long philosophical debates. You adore sharing your knowledge with others, and although you're a natural for pub quizzes you must resist any temptation to come across as a know-all.

You're instinctively laidback and relaxed and do your best to take life in your stride. What's more, your innate sense of optimism helps you to stay buoyed up when things go wrong, although sometimes you can tip over into feeling very bleak. Sagittarius is a sign that's renowned for its honesty, so occasionally you may struggle to be tactful and might at times even have foot-in-mouth syndrome. Never mind, because you're warm, affectionate, intelligent and great fun to be around, so you have a wide range of fans.

SUN IN ARIES, MOON IN SAGITTARIUS
Enthusiastic; warm-hearted; adventurous; risk-taking; energetic; competitive

SUN IN TAURUS, MOON IN SAGITTARIUS
Practical; inspired yet down-to-earth; stability contrasts with a need for adventure

SUN IN GEMINI, MOON IN SAGITTARIUS
Entertaining; intelligent; love of knowledge; restless; endlessly curious about the world

SUN IN CANCER, MOON IN SAGITTARIUS
Desire to stay close to home is tempered by the need to roam; loving; positive; friendly

SUN IN LEO, MOON IN SAGITTARIUS
Expansive; generous; extravagant; artistic; impatient; larger than life personality

SUN IN VIRGO, MOON IN SAGITTARIUS
Ability to focus on details and also see the bigger picture; changeable; restless; nervy

SUN IN LIBRA, MOON IN SAGITTARIUS
Charming; entertaining companion; persuasive; intelligent; loyal

SUN IN SCORPIO, MOON IN SAGITTARIUS
Thoughtful; ability to understand life's ups and downs; wide-ranging ideas

SUN IN SAGITTARIUS, MOON IN SAGITTARIUS
Open-minded; philosophical; fascinated by life; haphazard; hard to tie down

SUN IN CAPRICORN, MOON IN SAGITTARIUS
Thoughtful; keen intellect; serious yet playful; may combine work and travel

SUN IN AQUARIUS, MOON IN SAGITTARIUS
Spiritual quest; almost too honest; need for intellectual freedom; kind; humanitarian

SUN IN PISCES, MOON IN SAGITTARIUS
Flexible but can be unreliable; intuitive; compassionate; wide-ranging interests

Natal moon in Capricorn

If you were born with a Capricorn moon, here's some essential information to help you understand yourself. You can also use this to understand someone you know with the Moon in Capricorn. But the Moon doesn't work in isolation – the facing page tells you how your Moon fits with your Sun sign. You can also use this combination to discover how your Moon gets on with other Sun signs.

ELEMENT: **Earth**

MODE: **cardinal**

KEYWORDS: **structure, responsibility**

Life can be a serious business for you. It's not that you can't see the funny side of things, because you enjoy having a good laugh and your dry and wry sense of humour keeps others in stitches. But your strong sense of responsibility makes you always want to do the best you can, even when it means you lose out in some way. For instance, if an unpleasant or difficult task needs to be tackled, you may find that (yet again!) you've volunteered to sort it out, almost without realizing it. It's all because you have a strong need for stability and structure in your life, so living in chaos or being aware that something has been left unfinished is far more difficult for you than facing facts and getting on with whatever must be done. Even

so, you need to guard against the feelings of pessimism and anxiety that often lurk menacingly at the back of your mind, giving you a tendency to make heavy weather of problems. Sharing your thoughts and worries with trusted confidantes helps you to keep these feelings in proportion, though you won't open up to anyone if you suspect they might ridicule you.

When it comes to your emotions, you tend to play it cool. Big flashy displays of affection aren't your style, despite what you may be feeling deep inside. You're self-controlled and can be shy, so it doesn't take much to embarrass you in public. It may be a different story in private, though!

SUN IN ARIES, MOON IN CAPRICORN
Motivated; determined; needs a goal;
ambitious; Aries haste tempered by
Capricorn patience

**SUN IN TAURUS, MOON IN
CAPRICORN**
Grounded; down-to-earth; practical;
loyal; stubborn; need for reassuring
traditions

**SUN IN GEMINI, MOON IN
CAPRICORN**
Gemini quick thinking strengthened by
Capricorn common sense; a good
strategist

**SUN IN CANCER, MOON IN
CAPRICORN**
Family-minded; loyal and supportive to
loved ones; home-loving; conservative

SUN IN LEO, MOON IN CAPRICORN
Capable; organized; a quiet sense of
self-esteem; a need for respect and
recognition

**SUN IN VIRGO, MOON IN
CAPRICORN**
Precise; punctual; strongly dutiful and
responsible; can be a workaholic; prone
to worry

SUN IN LIBRA, MOON IN CAPRICORN
Hard-working; concerned about what
others think of them; needs to keep up
appearances

**SUN IN SCORPIO, MOON IN
CAPRICORN**
Still waters run deep emotionally;
reserved and private; sardonic sense of
humour

**SUN IN SAGITTARIUS, MOON IN
CAPRICORN**
Thirst for knowledge and experience;
deep thinking and philosophical;
fun-loving

**SUN IN CAPRICORN, MOON IN
CAPRICORN**
Self-contained; serious; reliable;
industrious; can be pessimistic; dry
humour

**SUN IN AQUARIUS, MOON IN
CAPRICORN**
Intelligent; Aquarian individualism can
be tempered by Capricorn reserve

SUN IN PISCES, MOON IN CAPRICORN
Piscean sensitivity balanced by
Capricorn practicality; must learn to
trust gut feelings

Natal moon in Aquarius

If you were born with an Aquarian moon, here's some essential information to help you understand yourself. You can also use this to understand someone you know with the Moon in Aquarius. But the Moon doesn't work in isolation – the facing page tells you how your Moon fits with your Sun sign. You can also use this combination to discover how your Moon gets on with other Sun signs.

ELEMENT: **Air**

MODE: **fixed**

KEYWORDS: **independent, humanitarian**

No one could accuse you of being sentimental or gooey. You can't bear lavish displays of emotion from other people, because that makes you feel slightly claustrophobic, and you prefer to keep a tight lid on your own feelings whenever possible. This makes you come across as slightly detached, cool and reserved, even when you're with those you love best. You have a wonderful gift for friendship, and there are plenty of people who want to be your friend, thanks to your offbeat sense of humour, your interest in others and your quirky view of the world. You're fascinated by ideas and may enjoy spending a lot of time ruminating on what makes people tick.

Two of your most important needs are the intellectual freedom to say what you think, even if that raises eyebrows or ruffles a few feathers, and enjoying your independence. You march to the beat of your own drum and fully believe that everyone is entitled to do things their way, too, so you struggle when you meet someone who wants to make you toe their particular line.

You also place great emphasis on telling the truth, even if your listeners don't like hearing it – an attitude that puzzles you. You have strong humanitarian instincts, with the innate urge to help your fellow humans, and also all the animal kingdom, in whichever way seems most appropriate to you.

SUN IN ARIES, MOON IN AQUARIUS
Enterprising; innovative; impatient;
desire for the truth can verge on
bluntness

SUN IN TAURUS, MOON IN AQUARIUS
Motivated; strong-willed; hard-working;
Taurean stability contrasts with
Aquarian rule-breaking

SUN IN GEMINI, MOON IN AQUARIUS
Quick-thinking; intelligent; fascinated
by people; uncomfortable with
emotional outbursts

SUN IN CANCER, MOON IN AQUARIUS
Cancerian emotions tempered by
Aquarian detachment; mothers their
friends; kind-hearted

SUN IN LEO, MOON IN AQUARIUS
Dignified; loving but can be self-
contained; artistic; loyal; fixed ideas can
lead to stubbornness

SUN IN VIRGO, MOON IN AQUARIUS
Logical and rational; clever; emotional
detachment provides protection from
the world

SUN IN LIBRA, MOON IN AQUARIUS
Entertaining; intrigued by people;
idealistic; Libran diplomacy clashes with
Aquarian honesty

**SUN IN SCORPIO, MOON IN
AQUARIUS**
Determined; steadfast; fixed ideas;
intransigent; emotions are intense but
not spoken of

**SUN IN SAGITTARIUS, MOON IN
AQUARIUS**
Honest but can be blunt; freedom-
loving; independent; searching for
life's truths

**SUN IN CAPRICORN, MOON IN
AQUARIUS**
Down-to-earth; Capricorn good sense
enlivened by Aquarian quirkiness; shy

**SUN IN AQUARIUS, MOON IN
AQUARIUS**
A true individual and can be eccentric;
strong humanitarian beliefs; emotionally
reserved

SUN IN PISCES, MOON IN AQUARIUS
Kind; generous; considerate; can be
naive; wants to save the world; artistic
and creative

Natal moon in Pisces

If you were born with a Pisces moon, here's some essential information to help you understand yourself. You can also use this to understand someone you know with the Moon in Pisces. But the Moon doesn't work in isolation – the facing page tells you how your Moon fits with your Sun sign. You can also use this combination to discover how your Moon gets on with other Sun signs.

ELEMENT: **Water**

MODE: **mutable**

KEYWORDS: **receptive, sensitive**

The combination of the emotional Moon and sensitive Pisces means that you're highly attuned to the atmosphere around you. You soak it up like a sponge, which can be lovely when you're somewhere beautiful but challenging when you're embroiled in a problematic situation or dealing with unpleasant people. It's almost as though you lack a layer of skin, making it difficult to protect yourself from the outside world. Being so impressionable and receptive can mean that you have psychic abilities; but it can also mean that you're suggestible and even gullible at times, especially when on the receiving end of a sob story. You're driven by a powerful blend of compassion and altruism, so you're eager to help others even when it's not in your best interests. It's important that you find ways to switch off from your own problems, as well as those of

others, so you can relax. However, escapism can be very tempting at times, although it can lead to more problems if you continue to avoid reality. On occasion the Moon in Pisces indicates someone who likes to be rescued from their problems, or who rescues others from theirs.

Everyone needs some peace and quiet, but you need it more than most. It's essential for your mental, emotional and spiritual wellbeing, and you may find that meditation, mindfulness or visualization is especially helpful when you need to completely relax.

SUN IN ARIES, MOON IN PISCES
Dynamism and energy tempered by
consideration and thoughtfulness;
idealistic; naive

SUN IN TAURUS, MOON IN PISCES
Practical; artistic; loving; strong need to
help others; romantic; easily hurt

SUN IN GEMINI, MOON IN PISCES
Changeable moods and ideas; highly
strung; intuitive; fascinated by people

SUN IN CANCER, MOON IN PISCES
Emotional; affectionate; moody;
intuitive; sensitive; attracts people who
need help

SUN IN LEO, MOON IN PISCES
Highly creative and artistic;
sophisticated; luxury-loving and can be
extravagant

SUN IN VIRGO, MOON IN PISCES
Virgoan efficiency complicated by
Piscean escapism; creative; kind;
self-sacrificing

SUN IN LIBRA, MOON IN PISCES
Romantic; sentimental; idealistic; artistic
and musical appreciation; dislikes
rocking the boat

SUN IN SCORPIO, MOON IN PISCES
Intuitive; psychic; chatty but always
holds something back; allure; charm;
mysterious

SUN IN SAGITTARIUS, MOON IN PISCES
Fascinated by life and people; love of
travel; optimistic; gregarious; generous

SUN IN CAPRICORN, MOON IN PISCES
Capricorn realism blends with Pisces
imagination; can be pessimistic;
emotionally vulnerable

SUN IN AQUARIUS, MOON IN PISCES
Idealistic; humanitarian; kind; Aquarian
coolness warmed by Pisces sensitivity

SUN IN PISCES, MOON IN PISCES
Vivid imagination; intuitive;
impressionable; empathic; dithery; can
be ungrounded

The eight lunar birth phases

During a lunar month, the Moon goes through eight different phases, each of which is determined by the specific number of degrees that separate it from the Sun. As each lunar month develops, we're able to see seven of these phases unfolding before us in the sky – weather permitting. However, an exact new moon is always invisible to us because it's blotted out by the Earth's shadow.

Each of these eight phases has an astrological significance, not only in our day-to-day activities but also when we consider the lunar phase in which we were born. That's because we came into the world carrying the energy of that particular phase and we strive to express it throughout our lives.

Your lunar phase Finding your natal lunar phase is easy. All you need to know are the Sun and Moon signs at the time of your birth, so you can understand the relationship between them.

Consult the Moon-sign finder on pages 26–9 to discover the sign that your Moon occupied on the day you were born. Write this down.

If you already know your Sun sign, write this down as well. If you were born on the cusp between one sign and the next, you can look up your exact Sun sign online with the help of a website that offers free chart calculations (see page 173).

Remembering that the zodiac runs from Aries to Pisces, work out whether your Sun is ahead of your Moon or your Moon is ahead of your Sun.

Count how many signs Sun and Moon are apart to find the lunar phase under which you were born. For instance, if you were born with the Sun in Aries and the Moon in Cancer, the Sun is ahead of the Moon and they are four signs apart in the first quarter phase. For the Sun in Capricorn and the Moon in Leo, the Moon is behind the Sun in the full moon phase.

New moon

 The Moon is between 0° and 45° ahead of the Sun, so between 0 and 1½ signs apart

Also known as a black moon, because it isn't visible, this is the phase when the Sun and Moon are together in the sky. As a result, it's as though the Sun and Moon share the same viewpoint, which means that you can have very strong opinions or be extremely subjective. Such a concentration of solar and lunar energy gives you plenty of energy, enthusiasm and impulsiveness, even though sometimes you run out of steam because you're trying to do too much.

Crescent moon

 The Moon is between 45° and 90° ahead of the Sun, so between 1½ and 3 signs apart

The Moon is waxing, and you have a lifelong urge to grow and develop in all sorts of ways. You're assertive and eager to get on with things. If you encounter any obstacles or snags, you won't let them defeat you. Instead, you'll work hard to find a way around them, thanks to your self-confidence. Sometimes you can feel pulled in two directions, torn between the stability offered by following a tried-and-tested approach and the excitement of doing things a bit differently. This is essentially a choice between the old and the new, and at times you can feel burdened by shadows from the past.

First quarter moon

 The Moon is between 90° and 135° ahead of the Sun, so between 3 and 4½ signs apart

At this stage in the lunar cycle there can be tension between the Sun and Moon, so you can feel at odds with yourself. One part of you wants to do one thing, while another part has a totally different objective. A good way of dealing with this is to take action, and you certainly don't like sitting around and waiting for things to happen. If you think a situation no longer serves you or is bogged down in the past, you have the urge to dismantle it and replace it with something newer and better. You need structure and enjoy creating frameworks on which you can build.

Gibbous moon

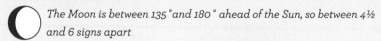

The Moon is between 135° and 180° ahead of the Sun, so between 4½ and 6 signs apart

You'll have a strong desire for personal growth throughout your life. You have a deep need to contribute something to the world, so that your life has a purpose and intention. It's as though you were born with a special mission that you have to fulfil; but you must be careful how you do this and avoid insisting that others follow your lead. You must also be wary of blindly following the ideas of others without thinking them through for yourself. When problems arise, you'll flourish and learn a great deal about yourself if you can work through those problems and find solutions.

Full moon

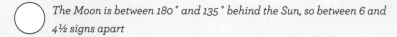

The Moon is between 180° and 135° behind the Sun, so between 6 and 4½ signs apart

This is the culmination of the Sun–Moon cycle, and if you were born during this phase you have the ability to set yourself targets and to reach them. You may even feel completely driven to do so sometimes. You have a good ability to blend practical considerations with your creative talents. Just as the full moon is so visible in the sky, you also need to be noticed and acknowledged. Relationships have immense significance for you, either because you're dependent on other people for your happiness and validation, or because you prefer to reject them and focus on yourself – unless you find someone who you consider to be perfect.

Disseminating moon

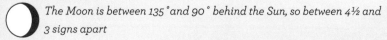

The Moon is between 135° and 90° behind the Sun, so between 4½ and 3 signs apart

The Moon is now separating from the Sun, and if you were born during this phase you have a deep urge to distribute your ideas and beliefs to other people. This can mean you get great pleasure from letting others know about the things that have had an impact on you and can even become a bit of a crusader when you feel strongly enough about something. You can be a marvellous teacher, whether you do that formally or informally. However, some people born into this phase can become fanatical or insist that they're the only person who's right.

Last quarter moon

The Moon is between 90° and 45° behind the Sun, so between 3 and 1½ signs apart

You have a maturity and wisdom that may belie your age. You might find this hard to believe because you're often engaged in an inner struggle over conflicts of interest. For instance, you might be very private yet also need to be with others and must find a way of balancing these two conflicting desires. You're caught up in ideological beliefs and need to live them out, which can trigger discord with others if they don't agree with you. It's important for you not to take yourself too seriously, to remain positive and constructive, and to be focused on the future.

Balsamic moon

The Moon is between 45° and 0° behind the Sun, so between 1½ and 0 signs apart

You have a contemplative and meditative nature. You can be quite a visionary at times, with mystical insights and a deep-seated need to be at one with nature. You may have a strong sense of intuition, with an ability to sense what the future will bring. Sometimes you may also feel a sense of social destiny or as though you're being led through life by something that is vastly bigger than you. Spirituality means more to you than material accomplishments, and your life may bring many changes as you pass from one chapter to the next. But each time this happens you learn something profound.

Working with new and full moons

Each new and full moon has something to tell us about what's happening in our lives, and also in the wider world, at the time those events occur. Their particular meaning is determined by the sign in which they fall. At a new moon, the sign is the one occupied by the Sun. At a full moon, the relevant sign is the one occupied by the Moon. The same is true of solar and lunar eclipses.

Sometimes a new or full moon, or an eclipse, seems to pass us by without much happening, while others mark a very significant phase of life. Why is this? When a new or full moon or eclipse makes a conjunction or opposition to one of the planets or four angles – Ascendant, Descendant, Medium Coeli (MC) or Imum Coeli (IC) – in our birth chart, this coincides with an important period in our life. The sign on the Ascendant describes someone's attitude to life; the sign on the Descendant shows what they want from relationships; the sign on the Medium Coeli shows what they are aiming for in life; the sign on the Imum Coeli describes their roots. This has the effect of lighting up our own chart and indicates a time when the area of affairs ruled by the planet or angle in question is highlighted.

Playing astrological detective

You can track these important times yourself – if you have a copy of your birth chart (easily available online if you don't want to consult an astrologer) – by looking to see when the upcoming new and full moons, and the eclipses, will make a conjunction or opposition to something in your natal chart over the coming year. Write these dates in your diary, then you can be particularly observant during those times, watching to see how each new or full moon or eclipse manifests for you. This is an excellent way of learning to understand how astrology works – you're seeing it in action, so you can begin to appreciate its subtleties.

You can look back at major events in your life and see whether they were described by the new and full moons and eclipses of the time. However, you should be aware that events around an eclipse can happen up to three months before the eclipse becomes exact, and up to three months afterwards. Sometimes, you may realize that the seed of the event was sown long before it came to fruition, so keep looking back at previous new and full moons and eclipses to see if they coincide with this starting point.

New moons

At a new moon, both the Sun and Moon focus their energy in one sign, so there's a huge concentration of solar and lunar power in one place in the zodiac. New moons are about beginnings, whether they're the first inklings of something completely new or a fresh phase in something that already exists. For instance, a new moon in Libra can indicate an entirely new relationship or a fresh chapter in an existing one.

Full moons

These are about endings, whether they signify something ending completely or simply the end of one phase in something that continues in a slightly different form. For instance, a full moon in Cancer can indicate a house move or an opportunity to sort out a domestic problem.

The Sun and Moon are 180° apart at a full moon, so the Moon occupies the opposite sign to that of the Sun. Full moons can create a build-up of tension, with the feeling that something's got to give; but it's helpful not to overreact or create a drama, even though that may be tempting.

Eclipses

A solar eclipse is a supercharged version of a new moon, just as a lunar eclipse is a supercharged version of a full moon. Eclipses carry so much extra power because of the precise alignment on the same plane of the Sun, Moon and Earth. The lunar nodes (see pages 68–71) are also involved in an eclipse, which some astrologers believe gives eclipses a fated quality.

Timing

The effects of a new or full moon are usually felt within two weeks of exactitude. Sometimes these effects pass quite quickly, but at other times the new or full moon may trigger a situation that takes a long time to resolve or is even life-changing.

An eclipse works differently, because its period of effect is spread out over three months on either side of the eclipse itself. The events after the eclipse may be a continuation of the initial events that happened before the eclipse or they may be other manifestations of the eclipse's main influence. For instance, a lunar eclipse in Capricorn may bring up situations that involve an older relative at first, followed by hard work towards an objective and having to deal with a responsibility – all events that come under Capricorn's rule.

You should never begin any important activity exactly at the time of a solar eclipse, or conclude anything exactly at a lunar eclipse, because the energy is so powerful that it can negate whatever it is you are trying to do. This is because eclipses symbolize the energy of the Sun (in a solar eclipse) or the Moon (in a lunar eclipse) being temporarily blotted out. Allow at least twenty-four hours to elapse after an eclipse is exact before taking action, and if possible, wait for thirty-six hours.

New and full moons in the twelve signs

Here's a brief list of possibilities for each of the signs in which new and full moons fall (whether or not they're eclipsed). These are starting points to trigger your imagination. When reading these suggestions, remember that new moons represent beginnings and full moons denote endings.

New or full moon in Aries Initiatives and enterprises; hastiness; excitement; focus on personal matters and appearance; military matters; sharp tools; anything to do with the head

New or full moon in Taurus Personal finances; values and priorities; sensuality; ownership; possessiveness; the beauty business; farming; obstinacy; anything to do with the throat

New or full moon in Gemini Communicating with others; short journeys; cars and bicycles; public transport; siblings; gossip; scandal; a busy time; buying and selling; anything to do with the hands, arms and lungs

New or full moon in Cancer Domestic life; family matters; nest-building; the home; parental concerns; nostalgia; home comforts; antiques; the past; anything to do with the breasts and stomach

New or full moon in Leo Creative or artistic activities; self-expression; drama in all its forms; children; love; gambling; enjoyment; pleasure; anything to do with the heart and spine

New or full moon in Virgo Health regimes or daily routine; day-to-day work; duty and service; colleagues; being organized and methodical; pets; detailed work; anything to do with the bowels

New or full moon in Libra One-to-one relationships, whether easy or difficult; teamwork; harmony; compromise; tact; charm; legal matters; indecision; anything to do with the kidneys

New or full moon in Scorpio Close or intimate relationships; sexuality; joint resources; taxation; jealousy; suspicion; life and death concerns; taboo topics; anything to do with the sexual organs

New or full moon in Sagittarius Broadening horizons; adventure; long journeys; travel of the mind or body; further education; publishing; philosophy; beliefs; anything to do with the hips and thighs

New or full moon in Capricorn Goals, career and winning the respect of others; responsibilities; authority figures; business matters; anything to do with the skeleton, knees and teeth

New or full moon in Aquarius Groups; kindred spirits; friends; hopes and dreams; independence; humanitarianism; technology; the internet; radical ideas; anything to do with the lower legs and ankles

New or full moon in Pisces Romance; escapism; work behind the scenes; secrecy; altruism; self-sacrifice; charities and voluntary work; institutions such as prisons or hospitals; anything to do with the feet

Timing in the garden

The rules about not taking any important actions at the time of a new or full moon, or an eclipse, also apply to gardening with the aid of lunar astrology. This is explained in part 5.

Lunar phase timing

It's fascinating to discover which lunar phase was operating at the time of your birth (see pages 54–7). But it can also be invaluable to watch the Moon's eight phases developing each month, because each phase has a special significance. Its prevailing mood, which is caused by its angular relationship with the Sun, has a huge influence on daily events. As you'll discover later in this book, timing some of your actions according to the phase of the Moon can be very helpful. Although not a guarantee of success, it certainly means that you're working *with* the energies of the Sun–Moon cycle, rather than against them. Tables showing the lunar phases between 2019 and 2032 are given in the back of the book.

New moon

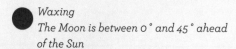 *Waxing*
The Moon is between 0° and 45° ahead of the Sun

Although the new moon presages beginnings, it isn't visible in the sky and therefore you don't yet have all the information you need to make a fresh start. You should be receptive to the idea that something new is starting, and trust your instincts, but not take action yet. Instead, use this energy to enjoy fun or creative activities.

Crescent moon

 Waxing
The Moon is between 45° and 90° ahead of the Sun

This is a good time to collect the information you'll need to make your new venture a success. You're starting to feel excited about what's coming up, and it's a good opportunity for networking and to begin making progress with your plans.

First quarter moon

Waxing
The Moon is between 90° and 135°
ahead of the Sun

You're capable of really solid progress, although it doesn't always come easily because there can be clashes with others. Even so, this phase is great for starting to take action, because you have lots of energy and are able to trust your gut instincts. You feel that you're finally starting to get somewhere, although this can still be a stressful time.

Gibbous moon

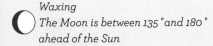

Waxing
The Moon is between 135° and 180°
ahead of the Sun

Pause to consider everything that you're currently dealing with, so you can make practical plans that will satisfy your own aims while also fitting in with the people around you. Try to stay focused, because this can be a period when you're easily distracted.

Full moon

Waning
The Moon is bewteen 180° and 135°
behind the Sun

At last, things are much clearer than they've been up to now. You have a better idea of what's happening and where you stand. Projects come to fruition. Relationships are highlighted, and as difficulties come to a head they can feel like a crisis. It's a good phase for being in the public eye and for socializing.

Disseminating moon

Waning
The Moon is between 135° and 90°
behind the Sun

This is a profound time, great for sharing your thoughts and ideas with others, especially if you're processing information that came to you during the full moon phase. You have a better understanding of some of the people in your life, and you're feeling creative and inspired. It's a good chance to revisit old projects.

Last quarter moon

Waning
The Moon is between 90° and 45° behind
the Sun

Take stock of where you stand and what's happening to you at the moment. It's a very busy phase, which can lead to tension at times, particularly if a project is reaching completion. You may also be reminded of the past, as people you once knew make contact with you again.

Balsamic moon

Waning
The Moon is between 45° and 0° behind
the Sun

Make this a quiet and reflective time, in preparation for the vibrant energy of the coming new moon. This is the end of a lunar cycle, so it's a good opportunity to catch your breath, enjoy the company of loved ones, relax and take pleasure in everything that you've achieved recently.

The 'void of course' moon

If you're interested in working with the Moon so you can choose the most effective time to do something and understand what sort of emotional weather each day will bring, you also need to know when the Moon isn't going to cooperate with you.

As you know by now, the Moon is the swiftest moving body in the solar system, moving out of one zodiac sign (each of which consists of 30°) into the next approximately every two-and-a-half days. While the Moon is in a particular sign, it will be creating aspects with some of the other members of the solar system. An aspect is a specific number of degrees that separates two planets (and remember that it's astrological shorthand to refer to the Sun and Moon as planets). Aspects are divided into two categories: major and minor. It's the major aspects that we're interested in here.

As soon as the Moon has made that final major aspect in a particular sign, it's said to be 'void of course'. You can look at this as meaning that the Moon has done its work in that particular sign and is now having the lunar version of a tea break before it moves into the next sign and starts making its next set of major aspects. The length of time that the Moon is void before moving into the next sign can vary dramatically. For instance, if the Moon makes its final major aspect when it's at 28° Sagittarius, it will only be void for four hours at most before it moves into Capricorn. But if it makes its final aspect at 6°, it will be 'void of course' for roughly two days.

Why does this matter?

The significance of a void moon

If we want to know when the Moon is at its most effective, we also need to know when it's not. When the Moon is void, the world doesn't fall apart but certain things are affected. In traditional astrology, when something is started during a void Moon it's said that 'nothing will come of the matter'. Any new venture begun under a void Moon will usually be unsuccessful or fizzle out at some point. If the venture does endure, it will need a lot of work and attention to ensure that it comes to fruition, at which point it may still be a disappointment. Therefore, it's best to treat these void periods with care.

When things aren't perfect

In an ideal world, all the lunar factors would slot into place like magic whenever we wanted to use the Moon's sign and phase to select the right time to do something. They would add up neatly to give us all the pointers we needed to time our actions for ultimate success.

But we don't live in an ideal world, and sometimes the Moon doesn't play ball in the way we'd like. For instance, the Moon might be in the most suitable sign for something you're planning, yet also be in an unsuitable lunar phase – or it might even be void. What do you do then?

Setting your priorities

The most important thing is to accept that we can't always get our astrological ducks lined up in the sort of Virgo-perfect row we'd like. Sometimes a few of those ducks refuse to behave themselves, so we have to make the best of what we've got, based on our priorities and the situation we're dealing with.

Let's say you want to throw a birthday party. Your actual birthday falls on a Saturday, which is ideal, but the Moon will be in staid and buttoned-up Capricorn and in the last-quarter phase. The atmosphere may be rather formal, instead of the jolly gathering you want, and your guests may feel tired and flat because of the lunar phase. The following Saturday, the Moon will be in Aries, which would make things much livelier, but it's just after a new moon so not all your guests may turn up. (Less light of the Moon means fewer people.) You've got to choose one of those dates, so which should it be? You need to decide whether you'd rather have a low-key party on your birthday, and perhaps make a virtue out of that by hosting an elegant cocktail party, or go for the high-spirited Moon in Aries day, knowing that not everyone might turn up.

A major consideration is always whether the Moon is void, because, as you now know, that can help to determine whether the actions you take at the time will come to anything. Sometimes this doesn't matter and might even be a bonus. Say you want to book a check-up with your dentist. You might decide to choose a day when the Moon is in the teeth-related sign of Capricorn, but on that day the Moon will be void. Do you want the dentist to give you a clean bill of dental health? Then the void moon could mean an event-free check-up and ensure you get exactly what you want.

Occasionally, it's clear that your options aren't suitable, and you need to postpone doing something until a more favourable lunar time. For instance, if you've got to choose whether to start a new venture during a void moon or a full moon, you may decide that the void moon is the most important consideration because of the danger that nothing will come from what you're doing. Yet starting something new at a full moon also runs the risk of the venture petering out before it makes any progress. Given these two difficult options, your best bet is to postpone the venture until a more favourable time, otherwise all your time and energy could be wasted.

Reading the signs

If you have no choice about the day an important event takes place, all you can do is check the sign and phase that the Moon will occupy, so you know the sort of things that could happen. For instance, maybe you've been invited to an interview for a job in a sales company. It would be brilliant if the Moon were in Gemini on that day, because that's one of the signs for sales work – however, the Moon is going to be in Libra. This tells you that it's a good day to focus on Libra-related actions, such as politeness and courtesy, as well as making sure that you look as well-groomed as possible. All of these things are going to count on this Libra-themed day. Libra is one of the signs connected to indecision, so make important choices ahead of time, such as planning your outfit and checking your journey to the interview, to ensure there's no Libran dithering on the day.

The North and South nodes

Do you ever wonder what your life is all about and what you're meant to be doing with it? The position of the Moon's North and South nodes at the time you were born will tell you. There's a list of these positions on pages 148–51, giving you the signs that they occupied at the time of your birth. If you'd like to know more about them, an astrologer will give you plenty of insights into their messages for you.

Where the Moon and Sun meet

As explained in part 1, the lunar nodes are formed at the points where the Moon's path crosses that of the Sun (see opposite). The two nodes are always 180° apart, so for instance if your North Node is in Gemini your South Node will be at exactly the same degree in Sagittarius. This relationship of 180° is called an 'opposition', because the two nodes share an axis and are striving for balance between the two signs involved. Every sign in the zodiac has various attributes that complement its opposite number, as you'll see in the descriptions of each nodal pairing that follows. The cycle of the lunar nodes is completed once every 18.6 years, with the nodes spending about eighteen months in each sign. They move backwards around the zodiac, from sign to sign, unlike all the planets, which move forwards.

The meaning of the nodes

There are various ways of looking at and interpreting the nodes. Some astrologers believe that they describe our previous lives, especially when we look in depth at the relationship they make to the rest of the natal chart. However, that's beyond the scope of this book. Here we're looking at

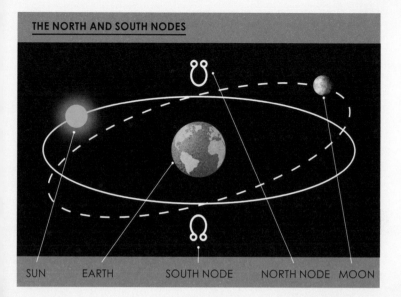

SUN   EARTH   SOUTH NODE   NORTH NODE   MOON

nodes as indicators of our fundamental purpose in life, with the North Node describing what we should be moving towards (not always easy because we may have some resistance to it or see it as uncharted territory) and the South Node showing what we should be moving away from (which can also be difficult because that position is familiar and can feel like a refuge). In each of the combinations below, you'll be able to see how the pairings of the signs affect one another. Each combination of signs describes two extremes that must somehow be made to work with one another, such as the methodical approach of Virgo and the chaotic and intuitive approach of Pisces.

How to work with the nodal pairings

The descriptions of the significance of each of the nodal pairings deal with some of their more obvious lessons, because they're intended to be an introduction to what is a very complex and profound branch of astrology. As you read about your particular pairing, bear in mind that the sign of your North Node shows what you're meant to be striving to attain in this life, and the South Node shows what may be comfortable for you but which must now be integrated into your quest to express the lessons of your North Node.

Aries–Libra With this pairing there's conflict between taking care of our own needs (Aries) and considering those of other people (Libra). We can't understand others (Libra) if we don't understand ourselves (Aries). We need to give ourselves the freedom to be who we really are (Aries) so we can allow others the freedom to be who they are (Libra). We need to cope with conflict and clashes with others (Aries) rather than always adopt the attitude of anything for a quiet life (Libra). Another lesson that this nodal axis teaches us is to balance our competitiveness and self-centredness (Aries) with our tendency to let others hold all the power (Libra).

Taurus–Scorpio Here there's a need for balance between what's ours (Taurus) and what we share with others (Scorpio). We must learn that when we can fend for and provide for ourselves (Taurus) we don't have to rely on others to do it for us (Scorpio). Another lesson is to express our sensuality, in all its forms (Taurus), without either denying it or letting it overwhelm us (Scorpio). We have to learn to immerse ourselves in the intensity of life's experiences (Scorpio) rather than play safe and cling to the status quo (Taurus). There must be a balance between profound personal transformation (Scorpio) and repeating the same patterns of behaviour again and again (Taurus).

Gemini–Sagittarius We must learn to express our beliefs and philosophies (Sagittarius) in ways that benefit our daily lives (Gemini). We must balance what can be fleeting interests (Gemini) with more deep-rooted concerns (Sagittarius). Also, we must investigate ideas without preaching or being arrogant (Sagittarius) while also not being glib or blasé about them (Gemini). Another lesson is to enjoy experiences with lively curiosity and interest (Gemini) while also understanding them at a deep level (Sagittarius).

Cancer–Capricorn There is a need for balance between sentimentality and an over-emotional outlook (Cancer) and an unemotional and overly stoical attitude (Capricorn). An emphasis on family life and the need for emotional security (Cancer) can vie with a desire to be noticed in the wider world and to gain the respect of our peers (Capricorn). Another lesson is to balance our instincts and gut feelings (Cancer) with strong self-discipline and self-control (Capricorn), and our emotional neediness (Cancer) with our need to protect our dignity (Capricorn).

Leo–Aquarius This nodal pairing highlights the need to be an individual and true to ourselves (Aquarius) while also fitting in with the people we care about (Leo). We must also balance our desire for romantic and personal love (Leo) with our desire to show love to humanity as a whole (Aquarius). There can also be lessons about having to find a happy medium between being caught up in our own life, with all its concerns (Leo), and being part of a larger group in which we might lose our sense of identity (Aquarius). Another lesson is to balance our need for independence and to be alone (Aquarius) with our need to be loved and admired by the people we care about (Leo).

Virgo–Pisces Here the task is to balance the desire to be useful and of service to others (Virgo) with the need to rescue them at all costs (Pisces). We must also find a compromise between our tendency to be critical of those we find wanting, which usually starts with ourselves (Virgo), and our idealistic tendency to put others on a pedestal (Pisces). We have to reconcile our need for order, rigidity and method (Virgo) with our need for chaos, fluidity and intuition (Pisces). Other lessons of this nodal placing include balancing our focus on the body (Virgo) with that of the spirit (Pisces), and complementing a tendency to compartmentalize every area of our life (Virgo) with an ability to tune into and merge with the vast universe (Pisces).

LOVE AND RELATIONSHIPS

Heaven or heartbreak? Let the Moon guide you through the pitfalls and practicalities of not only a happy love life but also a successful social circle, so you can zero in on the most auspicious days for relationships and steer clear of the ones that could cause trouble. Find out the best days for parties, first meetings, house moves and even marriage.

This section gives you the low-down on how to make the best of your relationships with the help of some invaluable lunar know-how.

3

My Aries moon and your moon

Aries moon and Aries moon Fast and furious; lively; argumentative; dramatic; funny; inventive; reckless

Aries moon and Taurus moon Encouraging; supportive; Aries spontaneity versus Taurean steadfastness; productive

Aries moon and Gemini moon Friendly; talkative; brimming with ideas and plans; flighty; fickle; fast-paced

Aries moon and Cancer moon Emotional; Aries independence versus Cancer dependence; mutually supportive; enterprising

Aries moon and Leo moon Exciting; enthusiastic; exuberant; good fun; daring; life-enhancing

Aries moon and Virgo moon Lack of understanding; quick-tempered; uncomfortable; hard-working; need for a shared aim

Aries moon and Libra moon A need for balance and mutual respect; challenging but rewarding; ambitious; sociable

Aries moon and Scorpio moon Temperamental; Aries shouting versus Scorpio sulking; shared energy and drive; sexy

Aries moon and Sagittarius moon Wide-ranging interests; undemanding; entertaining; always aiming high

Aries moon and Capricorn moon Excellent for business relationships; united in ambition; worldly; passionate

Aries moon and Aquarius moon Kindred spirits; Aries independence likes Aquarian originality; shared causes

Aries moon and Pisces moon Aries urgency clashes with Piscean hesitancy; challenging but educational; expressive

My Taurus moon and your moon

Taurus moon and Aries moon Encouraging; supportive; Taurean steadfastness versus Aries spontaneity; productive

Taurus moon and Taurus moon Reassuringly safe, with a shared need for physical and emotional security; can get bogged down in routine; hedonistic

Taurus moon and Gemini moon Enjoyable as friends; difficult as lovers if Taurean fidelity clashes with Gemini flirtatiousness

Taurus moon and Cancer moon Enjoyable, warm and satisfying; shared aims and a close understanding of each other's needs

Taurus moon and Leo moon Mutually supportive and encouraging; obstinacy can lead to stand-offs; passionate

Taurus moon and Virgo moon A shared respect for common sense and hard work; earthy and sexy lovers; close friends

Taurus moon and Libra moon Mutual affection; Taurean no-nonsense attitude can clash with Libran diplomacy

Taurus moon and Scorpio moon Profound understanding of each other's emotional needs; Taurean warmth makes Scorpio relax

Taurus moon and Sagittarius moon Taurean stability clashes with Sagittarian need for adventure; opposites can attract

Taurus moon and Capricorn moon Serious, committed and pragmatic; shared goals; powerful sexual chemistry

Taurus moon and Aquarius moon Taurean feelings can be hurt by Aquarian candidness; good as supportive colleagues or friends

Taurus moon and Pisces moon Taurean practicality helps Pisces to manifest dreams; loving and demonstrative friends or lovers

My Gemini moon and your moon

Gemini moon and Aries moon Friendly; talkative; brimming with ideas and plans; flighty; fickle; fast-paced

Gemini moon and Taurus moon Supportive friends; difficult as lovers if Taurean fidelity clashes with Gemini flirtatiousness

Gemini moon and Gemini moon Can talk themselves to a standstill; good fun; lively; possible lack of commitment

Gemini moon and Cancer moon Both can benefit, but Gemini need for space can upset the Cancerian need for a stable home life

Gemini moon and Leo moon Entertaining; sociable; bright and witty; devoted friends; always something new to discover

Gemini moon and Virgo moon Clever conversation; Gemini's casual approach can be at odds with Virgo perfectionism

Gemini moon and Libra moon Mutual respect; indecisive; can be scared of big emotional displays, taking refuge in ideas instead

Gemini moon and Scorpio moon Very talkative; fascinated by each other; Gemini's light touch can struggle with Scorpio intensity

Gemini moon and Sagittarius moon Bring out the best in each other; shared love of books and ideas; enterprising; freewheeling

Gemini moon and Capricorn moon Can struggle to understand each other; Gemini fluidity benefits from Capricorn motivation

Gemini moon and Aquarius moon Ideas and conversation galore; instinctive friends; shared need for independence

Gemini moon and Pisces moon Flexible; versatile; imaginative; sociable and chatty; Gemini may unwittingly hurt Piscean feelings

My Cancer moon and your moon

Cancer moon and Aries moon Emotional; Cancer dependence versus Aries independence; mutually supportive; enterprising

Cancer moon and Taurus moon Enjoyable, warm and satisfying; shared aims and a close understanding of each other's needs

Cancer moon and Gemini moon Both can benefit, but Gemini need for space can upset Cancerian need for a stable home life

Cancer moon and Cancer moon Great emotional rapport; must beware moodiness, defensiveness and competing family ties

Cancer moon and Leo moon Affectionate and loyal; shared love of home and family; traditional roles within the relationship

Cancer moon and Virgo moon Shared drive and goals; relaxed Cancerian approach can clash with Virgoan need for precision

Cancer moon and Libra moon Good as friends and lovers; strong loyalties; Cancer can feel threatened by busy Libra social life

Cancer moon and Scorpio moon Intuitive and sensitive; can be dramatic emotional scenes; sensual and sexy as lovers

Cancer moon and Sagittarius moon Intrigued by each other as friends; Cancerian security upset by Sagittarian need for freedom

Cancer moon and Capricorn moon Mutual understanding and support; shared motivation and drive for success; good fun

Cancer moon and Aquarius moon Chalk and cheese; can learn a lot from each other; loyal and supportive

Cancer moon and Pisces moon Emotional and sensitive; much can remain unspoken yet is understood; happy family life

My Leo moon and your moon

Leo moon and Aries moon Exciting; enthusiastic; exuberant; good fun; daring; life-enhancing

Leo moon and Taurus moon Mutually supportive and encouraging; obstinacy can lead to stand-offs; passionate

Leo moon and Gemini moon Entertaining; sociable; bright and witty; devoted friends; always something new to discover

Leo moon and Cancer moon Affectionate and loyal; shared love of home and family; traditional roles within the relationship

Leo moon and Leo moon Dramatic; demonstrative; mutual loyalty; egos can clash, with both needing to be in control

Leo moon and Virgo moon Mutually instructive; Leo learns patience and Virgo learns assertion; can be good friends

Leo moon and Libra moon Idealistic; romantic; complementary artistic sensibilities; shared appreciation of luxury

Leo moon and Scorpio moon Powerful; intense; dramatic; must guard against possessiveness and clashes of will

Leo moon and Sagittarius moon Great fun; plenty of laughter; shared love of travel, but Leo won't want to rough it

Leo moon and Capricorn moon Businesslike; shared need for status and respect; Leo warmth boosts Capricorn shyness

Leo moon and Aquarius moon Opposites attract; joint honesty; enjoyable social life; Leo can get jealous of Aquarius's friends

Leo moon and Pisces moon Shared love of the arts; kind and romantic; Leo encourages Pisces to be more self-assertive

My Virgo moon and your moon

Virgo moon and Aries moon Lack of understanding; quick-tempered; uncomfortable; hard-working; need for a shared aim

Virgo moon and Taurus moon A shared respect for common sense and hard work; earthy and sexy lovers; close friends

Virgo moon and Gemini moon Clever conversation; Virgo perfectionism can be at odds with Gemini's casual approach

Virgo moon and Cancer moon Shared drive and goals; Virgo need for precision can clash with relaxed Cancerian attitude

Virgo moon and Leo moon Mutually instructive; Virgo learns assertion and Leo learns patience; can be good friends

Virgo moon and Virgo moon Great working partners; witty conversations; worries shared can be worries doubled

Virgo moon and Libra moon Give and take needed; Virgo criticism can hurt Libran feelings; shared artistic appreciation

Virgo moon and Scorpio moon Shared goals as partners or colleagues; can be critical of each other; duty before pleasure

Virgo moon and Sagittarius moon Entertaining and clever; Virgo caution contrasts with Sagittarian love of adventure

Virgo moon and Capricorn moon Industrious; rational; shared belief in the value of hard work; very sexy behind the scenes

Virgo moon and Aquarius moon Shared love of ideas but can clash over opinions; more comfortable as friends than lovers

Virgo moon and Pisces moon Complementary needs; Virgo honesty can wound Pisces; excellent and inspired creative partners

My Libra moon and your moon

Libra moon and Aries moon A need for balance and mutual respect; challenging but rewarding; ambitious; sociable

Libra moon and Taurus moon Mutual affection; Libran diplomacy can clash with Taurean no-nonsense attitude

Libra moon and Gemini moon Mutual respect; indecisive; can be scared of big emotional displays, taking refuge in ideas instead

Libra moon and Cancer moon Good as friends and lovers; strong loyalties; busy Libra social life can make Cancer feel threatened

Libra moon and Leo moon Idealistic; romantic; complementary artistic sensibilities; shared appreciation of luxury

Libra moon and Virgo moon Give and take needed; Virgoan criticism can hurt Libran feelings; shared artistic appreciation

Libra moon and Libra moon Great mutual understanding; shared ideals; hearts and flowers; indecisive; wary of deep emotions

Libra moon and Scorpio moon Libran wariness of Scorpio intensity; both fascinated by ideas; must be honest with each other

Libra moon and Sagittarius moon Lively and interesting conversations; tactful Libra can be shocked by Sagittarian candour

Libra moon and Capricorn moon Excellent colleagues; shared goals; Libran feelings can be hurt by brisk Capricorn attitude

Libra moon and Aquarius moon Plenty to talk about; joint idealism can lead to dashed hopes; emotions are rationalized

Libra moon and Pisces moon Very sensitive; both easily hurt by the other; fantastic in joint artistic ventures; ultra-romantic

My Scorpio moon and your moon

Scorpio moon and Aries moon Temperamental; Scorpio sulking versus Aries shouting; shared energy and drive; sexy

Scorpio moon and Taurus moon Profound understanding of each other's emotional needs; Scorpio relaxes in Taurean warmth

Scorpio moon and Gemini moon Very talkative; fascinated by each other; Scorpio intensity can be baffled by Gemini's light touch

Scorpio moon and Cancer moon Intuitive and sensitive; can be dramatic emotional scenes; sensual and sexy as lovers

Scorpio moon and Leo moon Powerful; intense; dramatic; must guard against possessiveness and clashes of will

Scorpio moon and Virgo moon Shared goals as partners or colleagues; can be critical of each other; duty before pleasure

Scorpio moon and Libra moon Scorpio intensity can make Libra wary; both fascinated by ideas; must be honest with each other

Scorpio moon and Scorpio moon Great mutual understanding; can 'catch' each other's moods; emotionally intense

Scorpio moon and Sagittarius moon Shared interest in psychology and philosophy; wide-ranging conversations

Scorpio moon and Capricorn moon Shared work and personal goals; good business partners; raunchy behind closed doors

Scorpio moon and Aquarius moon Mutual respect; fascinated by each other; Aquarian detachment warmed by Scorpio intensity

Scorpio moon and Pisces moon Kindred spirits; on the same intuitive wavelength; emotional and affectionate

My Sagittarius moon and your moon

Sagittarius moon and Aries moon Wide-ranging interests; undemanding; entertaining; always aiming high

Sagittarius moon and Taurus moon Sagittarian need for adventure contrasts with Taurean stability; opposites can attract

Sagittarius moon and Gemini moon Bring out the best in each other; shared love of books and ideas; enterprising; freewheeling

Sagittarius moon and Cancer moon Intrigued by each other as friends; Sagittarian freedom can upset Cancerian need for security

Sagittarius moon and Leo moon Great fun; plenty of laughter; shared love of travel, but Leo won't want to rough it

Sagittarius moon and Virgo moon Entertaining and clever; Sagittarian love of adventure contrasts with Virgoan caution

Sagittarius moon and Libra moon Lively and interesting conversations; Sagittarian candour can shock tactful Libra

Sagittarius moon and Scorpio moon Shared interest in psychology and philosophy; all-encompassing conversations

Sagittarius moon and Sagittarius moon Endlessly chatty; wide-ranging conversations; good-natured competitiveness

Sagittarius moon and Capricorn moon Relaxed Sagittarian attitude can worry conscientious Capricorn; plenty to talk about

Sagittarius moon and Aquarius moon Joint seekers after life's truths; great companions; shared sense of humour

Sagittarius moon and Pisces moon Both adaptable and versatile; optimistic Sagittarius heartens cautious Pisces

My Capricorn moon and your moon

Capricorn moon and Aries moon Excellent for business relationships; united in ambition; worldly; passionate

Capricorn moon and Taurus moon Serious, committed and pragmatic; shared goals; powerful sexual chemistry

Capricorn moon and Gemini moon Can struggle to understand each other; Capricorn motivation is boosted by Gemini fluidity

Capricorn moon and Cancer moon Mutual understanding and support; shared motivation and drive for success; good fun

Capricorn moon and Leo moon Businesslike; shared need for status and respect; Capricorn shyness benefits from Leo warmth

Capricorn moon and Virgo moon Industrious; rational; shared belief in the value of hard work; very sexy behind the scenes

Capricorn moon and Libra moon Excellent colleagues; shared goals; brisk Capricorn attitude can hurt Libran feelings

Capricorn moon and Scorpio moon Shared work and personal goals; good business partners; raunchy behind closed doors

Capricorn moon and Sagittarius moon Conscientious Capricorn can be worried by relaxed Sagittarian attitude; plenty to talk about

Capricorn moon and Capricorn moon Supportive and encouraging; work and responsibilities can come between them

Capricorn moon and Aquarius moon Shared understanding, unless Capricorn is challenged by Aquarian forward thinking

Capricorn moon and Pisces moon Little in common, yet mutually beneficial because each has what the other lacks

My Aquarius moon and your moon

Aquarius moon and Aries moon Kindred spirits; Aquarian originality goes well with Aries independence; shared causes

Aquarius moon and Taurus moon Aquarian candidness can hurt Taurean feelings; good as supportive colleagues or friends

Aquarius moon and Gemini moon Ideas and conversation galore; instinctive friends; mutual need for independence

Aquarius moon and Cancer moon Chalk and cheese; can learn a lot from each other; loyal and supportive

Aquarius moon and Leo moon Opposites attract; joint honesty; enjoyable social life; Aquarius's social life can make Leo jealous

Aquarius moon and Virgo moon Shared love of ideas but can clash over opinions; more comfortable as friends than lovers

Aquarius moon and Libra moon Plenty to talk about; joint idealism can lead to dashed hopes; emotions are rationalized

Aquarius moon and Scorpio moon Mutual respect; fascinated by each other; Scorpio intensity warms Aquarian detachment

Aquarius moon and Sagittarius moon Joint seekers after life's truths; great companions; shared sense of humour

Aquarius moon and Capricorn moon Shared understanding, unless Aquarian forward thinking is too challenging for Capricorn

Aquarius moon and Aquarius moon Great friends but emotional reticence can lead to chilly spells; shared ideals and interests

Aquarius moon and Pisces moon An uneasy pairing if Aquarian emotional detachment damages sensitive Piscean feelings

My Pisces moon and your moon

Pisces moon and Aries moon Piscean hesitancy clashes with Aries urgency; challenging but educational; expressive

Pisces moon and Taurus moon Piscean dreams encouraged by Taurean practicality; loving and demonstrative friends or lovers

Pisces moon and Gemini moon Flexible; versatile; imaginative; sociable and chatty; Piscean feelings may be unwittingly hurt

Pisces moon and Cancer moon Emotional and sensitive; much is understood yet can remain unspoken; happy family life

Pisces moon and Leo moon Shared love of the arts; kind and romantic; Pisces encouraged by Leo to be more self-assertive

Pisces moon and Virgo moon Complementary needs; Pisces can be hurt by Virgo honesty; excellent and inspired creative partners

Pisces moon and Libra moon Very sensitive; both easily hurt by the other; fantastic in joint artistic ventures; ultra-romantic

Pisces moon and Scorpio moon Kindred spirits; on the same intuitive wavelength; emotional and affectionate

Pisces moon and Sagittarius moon Both adaptable and versatile; cautious Pisces heartened by optimistic Sagittarius

Pisces moon and Capricorn moon Little in common, yet mutually beneficial because each has what the other lacks

Pisces moon and Aquarius moon An uneasy pairing if sensitive Piscean feelings damaged by Aquarian emotional detachment

Pisces moon and Pisces moon Highly intuitive; empathic; can enlighten or confuse each other; must avoid joint escapism

First meetings

Astrology has so much to say about the first time we meet someone. If you look at the chart for that meeting in detail, you'll see all sorts of information about how your connection with each other will develop. Maybe it will flare up and then die out, or perhaps it will still be going strong years later.

Even knowing the sign occupied by the Moon when you meet someone for the first time will give you plenty of insight into how things will work out between you. This could be valuable information if you're arranging a blind date with someone. And don't forget that you can use this technique to investigate your current or past relationships as well, if you know the day when you first encountered one another.

Moon in Aries days Your first meeting could involve literally bumping into each other. Cars, military matters and even arguments might crop up. If you're attracted to each other it will be a fast, fiery and passionate affair, but may burn out as quickly as it began, especially if there's an element of idealism to it.

Moon in Taurus days You might connect over something relating to gardens, nature or the countryside. Finances might also bring you together, or you may share the same values or perspective on life. If you're looking for love, it will be sensual and sexy, but there could be problems about possessiveness.

Moon in Gemini days Chatter, chatter! There's plenty to talk about, and you love sharing ideas, as well as trading puns and jokes. Verbal wit could play a big part in your relationship. You may have met because of a school or local event. It's a flirty relationship, but the big question is whether it will last.

Moon in Cancer days Your first meeting may involve the sea, photography, nostalgia, antiques or domesticity, or you might both be avid collectors of something. You have a strong emotional connection, and it revolves around your home and family. The old-world atmosphere between you may come as a surprise.

Moon in Leo days Something dramatic or larger than life is going on when you first meet, so that first encounter could be really full-on. But once things calm down, you'll enjoy a loyal, loving and lasting relationship. You may meet first in a theatre or cinema, at an art gallery or in a creative workshop.

Moon in Virgo days It's quite likely that you'll meet at work or because of your daily routine. A health-related matter could also bring you together. Things may start off in a shy and hesitant fashion, with each of you waiting for the other to make the first move, but your relationship could develop into something special.

Moon in Libra days Fashion, the fine arts, a party or even the legal system could be the setting for your first meeting. You'll charm one another, and there could be plenty of old-style wooing to turn your head and win your heart. Expect a relationship filled with hearts and flowers, but not one as good at dealing with hard realities.

Moon in Scorpio days It may feel as though you were meant to meet each other, with some strange coincidences to marvel at or a fated quality to your first encounter. There's a deep bond between you, enabling you to discuss things you wouldn't normally talk about. There's also lots of passion.

Moon in Sagittarius days Long-distance travel, horses, further education or religion might be the reason for your first meeting, and once you get talking it will be a mind-stretching conversation, with many more to follow. You adore one another's love for life and sense of adventure. It's going to be fun!

Moon in Capricorn days Business, politics, responsibilities and government agencies might be the reason you meet, and you'll be eager to impress one another. Although you're reserved with each other at first, this relationship could become very passionate given time, so be patient and wait to see what develops.

Moon in Aquarius days You share an interest or hobby, or you might meet through a mutual friend, technology, in a futuristic environment or through a group activity. You're fascinated by the way each other's mind works, and even if you end up as long-term partners, you'll also be firm friends.

Moon in Pisces days There's a mysterious, romantic or otherworldly element to your first meeting, but there could also be confusion or crossed wires. Things aren't always what they seem, so tread carefully. If all goes well, this is an ultra-romantic and escapist partnership, full of compassion and empathy.

Finding a 'happy ever after'

As you'll know by now, whenever you're planning a big occasion it's a wise move to check what the Moon will be doing on the day in question. It's even more important to do this when you're arranging what you hope will be a once-in-a-lifetime event, such as moving in with someone, getting engaged or tying the knot. But it's not just beginnings that are influenced by the Moon. When you end a relationship, the ideal option is to consult the Moon's movements in advance so you can choose the right day for calling the whole thing off.

When you're thinking of making a big relationship commitment, you must always try to abide by the rules that follow. Sometimes it's not possible to tick off every item on this list because they won't coincide in the way you want, so you must be adaptable and look for the best possible combination of lunar factors.

Moving in together The Moon rules our homes, so if you want to stand a good chance of enjoying a happy home life with someone, whether it's a platonic flatmate or a romantic partner, you must make sure you get off on the right foot, astrologically speaking. The rules on pages 116–7 apply here, but you should also consider the following:

Choose a day when the Moon is in Taurus, Leo or Libra if you're moving in with a romantic partner.

Choose a day when the Moon is in Sagittarius or Aquarius if you're moving in with a friend.

Getting engaged Usually, engagements happen when one person pops the question and the other one – with luck – says 'yes'. So not only are you setting the tone of your future relationship when you tell someone you want to get engaged to them, you're also probably feeling nervous in case they say 'no'. You should consider the following:

- Make sure the Moon isn't void.

- Choose one of the Moon's waxing phases – preferably the crescent moon.

- Avoid the waning lunar phase, and especially the last quarter and balsamic moons.

- If you want hearts and flowers, choose a day when the Moon is in Taurus, Cancer, Leo, Libra or Pisces.

- If you prefer things to be understated and restrained, choose a day when the Moon is in Virgo or Scorpio.

Getting married For many people, this is perhaps the biggest life event, and they want to get it right. So, if you want to marry someone and you'd like it to be a memorable occasion for all the right reasons, here's what you need to consider:

- If nothing else, ensure that the Moon hasn't gone void. A void Moon can be bad news for a marriage, with either problems on the day itself or difficulties in the relationship afterwards.

- Choose a time when the Moon is waxing, focusing on the crescent moon and the early time of the gibbous moon.

- Avoid the day immediately on or after the new moon, or you may feel unsure about what you're doing.

- Avoid the days immediately after the full moon. Although you'll have lots of guests at your wedding, the lunar energy is waning – and the same may be said for your marriage.

- Decide on the sort of marriage you want and choose a suitable Moon sign. For instance, if you want a cosy, traditional marriage, opt for the Moon in Taurus or Cancer. If you want a more relaxed marriage in which you both keep your independence, go for the Moon in Aries, Gemini, Sagittarius or Aquarius.

Calling it quits As we all know, sometimes relationships don't work out in the way we want. If you know that a relationship is on its last legs, you can use the Moon as your guide to finding the right time to call a halt. This will help you to avoid a messy ending, thereby reducing the potential for bad feeling on both sides. Consider the following:

- Choose the waning phase of the Moon but wait for at least one day after the full moon is exact.

- Choose the last quarter Moon if you want this ending to be completely final and a clean break.

- Opt for a time when the Moon is void if you hope that your relationship will be resumed in the future, after you've both realized what you're missing.

- If you want the break-up to be as unemotional as possible, choose a day when the Moon is in Gemini, Virgo, Sagittarius or Aquarius.

- Hoping for a civilized split in which you both keep your dignity? Opt for a day when the Moon is in Leo, Libra or Capricorn.

- If you want to avoid future recriminations, steer clear of days when the Moon is in Taurus, Cancer or Scorpio.

Social success:

MONTHLY DOS AND DON'TS AT A GLANCE

MOON IN ARIES DAYS

DO
* ★ break the ice and get chatting to someone
* ★ make the first move, if that's appropriate
* ★ arrange to do something energetic or lively
* ★ go dancing
* ★ show your quick wit

DON'T
* ☆ be in too much of a hurry
* ☆ get embroiled in silly spats
* ☆ confuse love with lust
* ☆ idealize someone, in case you're disappointed later on
* ☆ arrive too early and then be annoyed at being kept waiting

MOON IN TAURUS DAYS

DO
* ★ make a big effort with your appearance
* ★ suggest spending time in a park, visiting a garden or walking in woodland
* ★ listen to music or visit an art gallery
* ★ buy someone (or yourself) some beautiful flowers
* ★ watch out for obstinacy

DON'T
* ☆ spend more money than you can afford
* ☆ eat or drink too much
* ☆ insist on always doing the same things
* ☆ be overtaken by possessiveness

MOON IN GEMINI DAYS

DO
* ★ network
* ★ listen to what others say
* ★ meet friends in a lively and bustling café or restaurant
* ★ arrange a neighbourly get-together
* ★ join a book group

DON'T
* ☆ get drawn into negative gossip
* ☆ keep checking your phone in public
* ☆ dominate the conversation with nervous chatter
* ☆ change your plans frequently, if that will inconvenience other people

MOON IN CANCER DAYS

DO
* ★ show your kind nature
* ★ offer to cook someone a delicious meal
* ★ get together with members of the family
* ★ give a loved one a big hug
* ★ follow your instincts

DON'T
* ☆ wallow in too much nostalgia
* ☆ watch a heartrending film or play that leaves you a tearstained mess
* ☆ be drawn into recriminations about the past
* ☆ practise smother-love
* ☆ go into a bad mood at the first hint of a problem

MOON IN LEO DAYS

DO
* ★ be charming
* ★ draw other people out
* ★ let others see how warm and friendly you are
* ★ express your true personality
* ★ enjoy acting, dancing or singing

DON'T
* ☆ feel undermined when someone brags about their possessions or greatest achievements
* ☆ be extravagant if you can't afford it
* ☆ name-drop to impress others
* ☆ want to have everything your own way
* ☆ let anyone boss you about

MOON IN VIRGO DAYS

DO
* ★ get together with colleagues
* ★ check no one is allergic to the food you may be offering
* ★ have a good laugh with someone
* ★ avoid anyone who's often critical of you
* ★ make time for fun

DON'T
* ☆ obsess over tiny details that then start to loom large
* ☆ cancel a date so you can catch up on your workload
* ☆ tell horror stories about your health problems or those of a friend or relative
* ☆ allow your social life to slip into a dull routine

MOON IN LIBRA DAYS

DO

★ use your charm

★ be diplomatic

★ opt for one-to-one events rather than group gatherings

★ go somewhere with cultural or artistic connections

★ watch a romantic film

DON'T

☆ be indecisive about social arrangements

☆ accept an invitation out of duty

☆ mix with someone who's often rude or brash

☆ put a loved one on a pedestal

MOON IN SCORPIO DAYS

DO

★ speak kindly and from the heart

★ enjoy activities with a mysterious or intriguing slant

★ engage with your deepest emotions

★ read a ghost story aloud during a cosy evening by the fire

★ listen to music that touches your soul

DON'T

☆ badger someone into divulging a secret

☆ try to control a situation or dictate terms

☆ give way to simmering resentment

☆ let intense emotions get the better of you

☆ feel jealous of a lover or friend

MOON IN SAGITTARIUS DAYS

DO

★ get together with people who share your enthusiasms

★ go on a long-distance journey

★ mix with someone from a different culture or country

★ eat food that you find exotic

★ plan a forthcoming holiday or mini-break

DON'T

☆ be honest to the point of bluntness

☆ exaggerate to make a point

☆ insist that others agree with your opinions

☆ take foolish risks

☆ drive too fast

MOON IN CAPRICORN DAYS

DO
- ★ take responsibility for your actions
- ★ make contact with someone you respect
- ★ watch or read something that tickles your funny bone
- ★ mix business and pleasure
- ★ relax and have some fun

DON'T
- ☆ be late – you won't be popular!
- ☆ let shyness get the better of you
- ☆ try to be someone you're not
- ☆ go overboard when dressing to impress
- ☆ ignore someone because they're from a different generation

MOON IN AQUARIUS DAYS

DO
- ★ be your unique self
- ★ take part in a group activity
- ★ relax with a favourite hobby or pastime
- ★ hatch an exciting plan with a friend
- ★ make a humanitarian gesture

DON'T
- ☆ be standoffish
- ☆ take independence to an extreme
- ☆ always play by the rules
- ☆ be scared off by someone's eccentricity
- ☆ let cool rationality override your emotions

MOON IN PISCES DAYS

DO
- ★ double-check the arrangements for a social event in case they've got scrambled
- ★ be charitable
- ★ attend a concert or ballet
- ★ give someone a treat
- ★ unleash your inner romantic

DON'T
- ☆ be a Cinderella in the kitchen while everyone else enjoys themselves
- ☆ dither instead of making a decision
- ☆ idealize someone and imagine that they're perfect
- ☆ let your heart rule your head on every occasion
- ☆ allow anyone to put you down

WORK AND MONEY

Want to make a big splash at work or find the perfect career? The Moon can point you in the right direction, not only by revealing what makes you happy at work but also telling you when to apply for a new job. Moon power is invaluable, too, when making financial decisions, whether that's buying or selling, investing or signing on the dotted line.

Because the Moon describes our instincts and what's familiar to us, it plays an extremely important role at work. It influences the sort of colleague we make, as well as the type of working conditions we want.

The Moon and you at work

The Moon describes what's habitual and familiar to us. So although it doesn't tell you the sort of job that suits you best, the sign that it occupied when you were born does says a lot about the areas you might enjoy, your abilities at work, the type of colleague you make and the working conditions that you find comfortable.

Natal moon in Aries You need room and space to breathe at work. Being self-employed is ideal, because you have the courage and energy to make a success of working for yourself. There are several things you can't stand, including being told what to do, being ignored when you have a good idea and jobs that are brain-numbingly repetitive. You're great at starting things but not so good at finishing them, so you need someone else to do that for you. Lively and busy surroundings suit you, with plenty of people to chat to when you feel like it. Although cooperating with others can be a struggle, you enjoy being part of a team, but only if you're a leader, not a minion.

Natal moon in Taurus Hot-desking? Forget it! Anything temporary is your idea of a nightmare. You need a steady, reliable routine in familiar and attractive surroundings, with people you can get to know on a long-term basis. That's when you can relax and show yourself at your best –

which really is saying something, because you excel at hard, determined work. You have tremendous sticking power and hate to let others down by not doing things properly. It can take a while for you to become comfortable with a new regime or even a new workmate, because change unsettles you. You're a loyal and supportive colleague and will gladly let a favoured few share the edible treats stored in your desk drawer or locker.

Natal moon in Gemini A boring or dreary job in which you can't tell one day from the next is the very last thing you're looking for. You're much happier in working conditions that are busy, buzzy and with plenty of variety. Your great communication skills make you a natural for working with the public, or in negotiations or sales. Anything connected with the written word suits you, too, and you love the latest technology. Versatility and adaptability are two of your greatest strengths, and your job must reflect that, otherwise stagnation will always be looming on the horizon. Colleagues who like a good gossip, and who share your intelligence and sparkling wit, are also essential for you to be happy at work.

Natal moon in Cancer As with so many other areas of your life, you need a job that offers you emotional security, plus the reassurance that you're valued and part of a close-knit team. Working alone may not suit you, because you love the friendship and companionship of colleagues. You do your best to be a supportive, kind and friendly teammate, and love to stash away chocolate or biscuits to share with anyone who seems in need of comfort. Any job that involves showing empathy, caring for others or working with babies and children is ideally suited to you. Another good option is to work with food, whether you're growing, cooking, selling or serving it.

Natal moon in Leo Regardless of the work you choose, you need to do something that allows you to shine. Your Leo moon hates to be ignored, overshadowed or taken for granted. You have fabulous organizational skills; so, working for people who are incompetent won't suit you at all. Subservience won't suit you either, because you have natural authority – although you must watch out for a tendency to become bossy and believe your own publicity. Ideally, you need a job that enables you to express your many creative and artistic talents, especially in an area of the arts. Your sociable nature means you need some convivial colleagues, too.

Natal moon in Virgo Being of service to others is as natural to you as breathing, so you're instinctively drawn to jobs that involve taking care of people. This can be anything from nursing to catering, or simply being the person that your colleagues turn to in a crisis. You're responsible, practical and methodical, and may even have a formidable talent for creating filing systems and other organizational schemes. Despite this, your innate modesty means you can feel daunted by tasks that seem too ambitious for you. Perhaps you're underestimating yourself? Watch out for workaholic tendencies, which may mean you end up toiling round the clock and wearing yourself out.

Natal moon in Libra Working with people you like is a really important part of any job for you. If your colleagues are on the same intellectual wavelength as you, then so much the better, because you love sharing ideas. One thing you definitely can't cope with is being caught in the middle of warring factions, such as having to work with people who are always arguing, because you're only happy in a harmonious working atmosphere. You may also struggle if you spend too much time working alone, because of your need to have others around you, so could end up spending a lot of time chatting on the phone. Jobs in the beauty or fashion business, or involving some form of legal work or diplomacy, suit you.

Natal moon in Scorpio Thanks to the emotional depths of your moon, and all the experience this brings, it takes a lot to shock you. You may even have been through the mill several times yourself, so you know what it's like at first hand. This means you're a natural for any work that involves helping people in crisis, especially if it's the sort of crisis that society thinks is taboo, perhaps involving bereavement, drugs or sex. You're also skilled at psychotherapy or counselling, thanks to your great understanding of the human psyche. At work, you form intense connections with a few carefully chosen colleagues, rather than light-hearted friendships with everyone.

Natal moon in Sagittarius Your warm, gregarious nature makes you the perfect choice for any job that involves encouraging other people in some way. You're fascinated by facts and never stop learning, with an innate ability to share your knowledge and enthusiasm with all sorts of people. This means you're a natural teacher or lecturer. You're also fascinated by work involving travel, languages, publishing, religion or spirituality. It's important for you to have a job that gives you plenty of variety and room to grow, with good prospects for promotion. You enjoy the challenges of being your own boss but may need someone to help you keep track of all the paperwork!

Natal moon in Capricorn You believe in hard work and effort, often to the point of overdoing it. Partners and friends who rarely see you because you're so busy may have accused you of being a workaholic, and in your heart of hearts you agree with them. Not only do you like to know that you've done a job properly, you also have a strong work ethic and find it hard to relax if you know

there's something you ought to be doing. Colleagues and employers can rely on you, thanks to your organizational skills, your punctuality and your ability to meet deadlines. Any work involving responsibility suits you, but especially something related to business, architecture or banking.

Natal moon in Aquarius Fitting into a traditional nine-to-five working environment may be a step too far for you. For a start, you hate having to stick to a rigid routine, preferring to be more flexible. And you may also struggle with having to do what you're told, especially if you have a low opinion of the abilities of the person giving you the orders and are convinced you could do things so much better. You're a great colleague but aren't always happy as an employee, so self-employment suits you well. You're drawn to technology, computers and engineering, and also jobs with a humanitarian emphasis.

Natal moon in Pisces Your ideal job is more of a vocation than something that pays the bills. You need to feel involved in what you're doing, particularly if it enables you to help others by giving them your empathy, sensitivity and compassion. There could be a spiritual element to your work, too, even if it isn't immediately apparent. Your strong intuition enables you to tune into colleagues, bosses and customers, and ideally, they should be kindred spirits. This means you need to work in a peaceful atmosphere. Facing up to work problems can be a challenge, but avoiding them can lead to more problems in the long run.

Job-seeking with the Moon

One of the Moon's roles is to influence our everyday lives, so it's an important factor when looking for a job. You need to ensure that you're doing it on the right days if you want your job-seeking activities to be in tune with the Moon's mood. That's true of days when you're going to a job interview, too.

Moon in Aries days Be sure to read the job details carefully, rather than scan them quickly and then hope for the best. At the interview, try not to be in too much of a hurry to answer questions or to gloss over important points.

Moon in Taurus days You'll want to make sure you've done everything properly, but do give yourself some leeway for a little spontaneity. At the interview, show that you're dependable and reliable, but also warm and engaging.

Moon in Gemini days Your thoughts may be going in several directions at once, so it's important to keep track of what you're doing, writing or saying. Make the most of your intelligence and wit and show that you can be versatile.

Moon in Cancer days You're feeling more emotional than usual, so could have inexplicable gut reactions to what you say or do, or the people you meet at the interview. Stay upbeat and don't be fazed if someone comes across as moody.

Moon in Leo days You have a strong sense of pride about what you've achieved, but don't let it make you seem big-headed or boastful. In an interview, let others talk when necessary, even if you don't agree with what they're saying.

Moon in Virgo days Details are key, so make sure you've got everything covered – but not to the point of obsession. Make sure you look neat and smart if you're going to an interview and stay calm so that nerves don't get the better of you.

Moon in Libra days Emphasize your charm and diplomatic skills, as well as your ability to see two sides to every story. However, watch out for indecisiveness that makes you doubt your choices or wastes valuable time.

Moon in Scorpio days The atmosphere can be tense, so try not to let this get to you, whether you're working on your CV or attending an interview. Your intuition is strong, but you must stop short of reading too much into every comment or glance.

Moon in Sagittarius days You're feeling relaxed, which is great for being at ease in an interview; but beware of seeming slapdash or blasé. Show your sense of humour if it's appropriate but take things seriously when necessary, too.

Moon in Capricorn days Banish your nerves and doubts and remind yourself of why you'd be so good for this job. Emphasize your sense of responsibility; but you need to show your lighter side too, so don't just focus on your ability to work hard.

Moon in Aquarius days Concentrate on the qualities and interests that make you unique, while also showing that you can be part of a team. Allow extra time when travelling to an interview in case of delays or other unexpected events.

Moon in Pisces days Stay focused on the essentials; otherwise you'll be easily distracted. Double-check your CV and job application before sending them off. Watch out for an idealistic approach that makes you brush aside difficult topics.

Key points to remember

- Don't look or apply for jobs on days when the Moon is void or eclipsed – and try to avoid those days for interviews too.

- Submit your job application in the period between a new and a full moon, starting one day after the exact new moon and stopping one day before the exact full moon.

At work with the Moon

Each Moon sign focuses on particular energies and tells you which areas to concentrate on at work. So, let the Moon help you to be at your most efficient at work as it makes its progress across the zodiac each month. The sign occupied by the Moon on a particular day will give you a good idea of how best to harness its energies.

Moon in Aries days Take action! Be enterprising, start a new project, take the initiative and show what you can do. It's exciting to be on the ball but beware of overestimating your abilities or making hasty decisions in the heat of the moment. You must also guard against getting embroiled in bad-tempered encounters with others.

Moon in Taurus days Be practical and grounded and take a tried and tested approach rather than branch out in a new direction. In other words, you need to play it safe and focus on your strengths. The pace of life may be slower than normal, and you won't be able to speed things up. It's a chance to make considered decisions, but not to be lazy.

Moon in Gemini days Negotiations, meetings, conversations, emails and texts are emphasized, because it's a great time to communicate with other people. It also pays to be versatile and flexible whenever possible, so be open to fresh ideas and last-minute changes of plan, or to working on more than one project at a time. Try not to lose too much time in idle chit-chat.

Moon in Cancer days Don't be surprised if people at work are more emotional or moody than normal. Of course, you may also be swayed by your feelings. It's a good opportunity to create a cosy atmosphere with colleagues, as though you're one big happy family. Any work connected with food, domestic life and the past, as well as nostalgia and antiques, should go well.

Moon in Leo days You long to make a splash and grab other people's attention – you'll hate it if you think you're being sidelined or ignored. Jobs involving fashion, drama and other creative professions are highlighted, and you may feel inspired to showcase your particular talents and flair. Love – platonic or passionate – could also liven things up at work.

Moon in Virgo days Meticulous planning, taking care of details, analytical thinking and being organized are the four key activities. You want to do your very best, but make sure you don't work yourself into the ground, which is a possibility if you start to worry that you aren't doing enough. Jobs involving health, hygiene and being of service to others all benefit from this lunar influence.

Moon in Libra days Teamwork is of the essence. It's a time to pair up with others, even if that only means having lunch with someone. You're keen to create harmony, which may involve pacifying others or putting up with someone's rudeness; so, you'll be reluctant to ruffle feathers. Work connected with the legal system, beauty industry, interior design and human resources do well.

Moon in Scorpio days What's happened to the relaxed atmosphere at work? People could be cagey with you, or even downright suspicious, and you may suspect that there are secrets you don't know about. Even so, it's a marvellous time for intense conversations or for working behind the scenes. Jobs involving psychotherapy, research, tax and taboo subjects are all highlighted.

Moon in Sagittarius days This is a great time to make expansive and enterprising plans, although if they're too optimistic they may not see the light of day. The travel industry, further education, equestrian pursuits and publishing all benefit from this influence. You're eager to be honest but a little tact may be necessary, too. Beware of being clumsy.

Moon in Capricorn days It's time to adopt a conservative and considered approach. You're taking everything seriously, so tasks may seem more daunting than normal. A lack of confidence may make you doubt yourself, yet you need to feel that you're earning other people's respect. Work connected with big business, officialdom, architecture or government is highlighted.

Moon in Aquarius days Who cares about doing things by the book? You long to branch out, try something different and raise a few eyebrows. Taking the lead and being original – and possibly even eccentric – all appeal to you, and you may even feel totally inspired to do your own thing. Jobs that involve technology, IT, humanitarian work and the future all do well.

Moon in Pisces days Take care of yourself, because everything may feel like more effort than normal. You're highly sensitive to atmospheres, which may mean that your intuition is bang on target or that you're reading too much into a situation. Work involving the sea, the perfume business, the oil industry, fishing or institutions is affected by this influence.

Managing your money

Although the Moon doesn't rule money in the horoscope – that's the province of Venus – tracking its movement through the different zodiac signs and lunar phases will give you a good indication of how to handle your finances from day to day. Remember to avoid starting anything new, or signing any documents, on a day when the Moon is void, although it's OK to review existing arrangements on these days.

Bargain-hunting

We all love snapping up a bargain, but we need to choose the right day to do it.

- Hunt out bargains on days when the Moon is waning in Virgo, Scorpio or Capricorn.

- Negotiate the price or get involved in bartering when the Moon is in Aries or Gemini.

- Don't believe everything you're told about an incredible bargain on days when the Moon is in Gemini, Libra, Sagittarius or Pisces. It's probably too good to be true.

Contracts and agreements

It's important to choose the right lunar day and phase when issuing or signing contracts or agreements, especially if they will be legally binding for a long time to come.

- Draw up contracts in the period between the day after a new moon and the end of the first quarter phase.

- Avoid writing, issuing or agreeing contracts at the time of a solar or lunar eclipse.

- Negotiate the terms of an agreement or contract when the Moon is in Gemini or Libra.

- Carefully read the small print before signing documents on days when the Moon is in Virgo or Capricorn.

- Avoid signing documents on days when the Moon is in Aries or Pisces, or during the new moon phase, because you may have overlooked something important.

- Close a deal or reach an agreement between the full moon and last quarter phases, and when the Moon is in Taurus, Scorpio or Capricorn.

- Cancel an agreement or contract when the Moon is between the last quarter and balsamic phases.

Investments

It doesn't matter whether you're investing a small fortune or a tiny amount, because the astrological rules are the same.

- The best time to make any sort of investment is when the Moon is waxing, and preferably in the crescent or first quarter phases.

- If you're not sure whether to go ahead with an investment, assess the situation at the time of a gibbous or full moon.

- Be sure to avoid any action at the time of either a solar or lunar eclipse.

- Don't let anyone pressure you into making decisions on days when the Moon is in Pisces or there is a new moon, because you may not yet have all the details.

- Resist the temptation to believe someone's hard-sell approach on days when the Moon is in Aries, Sagittarius or Pisces.

- Ask searching questions on days when the Moon is in Virgo or Scorpio, and during the gibbous and full moon lunar phases.

- Avoid making an investment during any of the Moon's waning phases, otherwise your investment may drop in value.

- Seek professional financial advice during the first quarter or gibbous phase of the Moon, and when the Moon is in Taurus, Scorpio or Capricorn.

Banking

Here are a few guidelines to help you get the best out of your bank.

- Open a personal account, or check the details of your account, when the Moon is in Taurus.

- Open a joint account, or check the details of your account, when the Moon is in Scorpio.

- Open an account when the Moon is waxing.

- Close an account when the Moon is waning between the last quarter and balsamic phases.

- Contact a bank to ask questions when the Moon is in Taurus, Virgo, Scorpio or Capricorn.

- Apply for a loan when the Moon is in Scorpio and waning between the last quarter and balsamic phases.

- Apply for a mortgage when the Moon is waning in Cancer.

Work and financial management:

MONTHLY DOS AND DON'TS AT A GLANCE

MOON IN ARIES DAYS

DO

★ snap up bargains in the sales

★ have the courage to negotiate the price

★ say you'll think about something if you're not sure whether to go ahead with it

★ be prepared to walk away from a bad deal

DON'T

☆ make rash decisions at work

☆ get annoyed if things don't go your way

☆ imagine that if something doesn't fit you in the shop it will magically become the right size when you get it home

☆ tell other people what they should be doing

MOON IN TAURUS DAYS

DO

★ buy items made from beautiful materials

★ spend your own money

★ buy yourself an indulgent treat

★ look for value for money

★ make practical decisions about your own money

DON'T

☆ lend something if you're not completely happy to do so

☆ get involved with anyone who wants to control your decisions

☆ place too much emphasis on materialism and money

☆ insist on doing things a certain way or not at all

☆ behave as if everyone shares your set of priorities

MOON IN GEMINI DAYS

DO

★ write a blog or press release

★ negotiate a price or a deal

★ write important letters or emails

★ buy a bicycle, motorbike or car

★ take an active role in meetings

DON'T

☆ gloss over the facts because you think they're boring

☆ get talked into doing something against your better nature

☆ spend too long gossiping at work and not enough time working

☆ become sidetracked by social media sites

MOON IN CANCER DAYS

DO

★ buy items for your next beach holiday

★ shop for presents for your family or close friends

★ create a cosy and safe atmosphere at work

★ spend money on food and other domestic items

★ work on anything connected with buying or renting a house

DON'T

☆ make any financial decisions that are based purely on nostalgia

☆ hold on to anything or anyone that no longer has a place in your life

☆ allow your decisions to be solely influenced by your mood

☆ go into a huff when someone doesn't agree with you

MOON IN LEO DAYS

DO

★ invest in luxury goods such as gold

★ buy yourself a treat

★ unleash your organizational talents at work

★ work on a creative project

★ get busy on publicity and PR tasks

DON'T

☆ buy anything simply because it's a status symbol

☆ go shopping if you're feeling broke

☆ allow anyone to undermine you

☆ show off about your past triumphs

☆ let your extravagant mood drain your bank account

MOON IN VIRGO DAYS

DO

★ invest in your health and wellbeing

★ buy clothes or items for your job

★ pay attention to small details

★ stick to a strict budget

★ pay attention to your workmates

★ provide service with a smile

DON'T

☆ go on a spending spree – you won't be in the mood to fritter away your money

☆ worry about the things you can't control

☆ take on too much work and wear yourself out

☆ forget to have a short break every now and then

MOON IN LIBRA DAYS

DO

★ buy items made from beautiful materials

★ buy something fashionable or elegant

★ be courteous in meetings and allow everyone to have their say

★ make a big effort with someone who's often difficult to deal with

★ encourage people to negotiate

DON'T

☆ give someone a present in the hope that it will make them like you better

☆ feel you have to buy something because it's the polite thing to do

☆ consider so many options that you can't make up your mind about any of them

☆ keep quiet about something important for fear of causing offence

MOON IN SCORPIO DAYS

DO

★ focus on joint ventures and resources

★ be wary of anyone who won't tell you the facts or who's keeping something secret from you

★ decide how much money to spend in advance

★ carry out in-depth research

DON'T

☆ become overly suspicious of others

☆ get involved in any revenge tactics

☆ feel jealous of someone else's success

☆ disguise the fact that you feel strongly about something

MOON IN SAGITTARIUS DAYS

DO

★ buy tickets for a long-distance journey

★ invest in a holiday

★ buy books and reference material

★ listen to the opinions of colleagues and customers

★ rise to a challenge

DON'T

☆ exaggerate the facts to make them sound more convincing or to grab someone's attention

☆ overlook small but important details

☆ forget to have a good laugh so you can relax

☆ be slapdash or careless

MOON IN CAPRICORN DAYS

DO

★ think carefully before making a financial commitment

★ buy items that you hope will create a good impression, especially for work or an upcoming job interview

★ buy a watch or clock

★ attend to your responsibilities

★ earn others' respect by showing how capable you are

DON'T

☆ let fear or anxiety stop you making constructive decisions

☆ spend an excessive amount of time at work or doing your duty

☆ make a rod for your own back at work

☆ be self-defeatingly modest

MOON IN AQUARIUS DAYS

DO

★ think outside the box

★ ask awkward questions if they're appropriate

★ join a club or other group of kindred spirits

★ come up with some original ideas

★ approach problems from a fresh angle

DON'T

☆ be browbeaten by anyone who insists that they have all the answers

☆ make impulsive purchases simply because you're bored and want to distract yourself

☆ become too emotionally detached from colleagues

MOON IN PISCES DAYS

DO

★ make a donation to a charity or another good cause

★ buy shoes or boots, or spend money on anything else connected with your feet

★ keep the receipt in case you need to return something

★ be kind to colleagues and customers

★ trust your intuition

DON'T

☆ let anyone bully you into making a decision

☆ spend money you haven't got

☆ overlook your bank or credit card statement

☆ get too distracted at work

☆ ignore your instincts and hunches

AT HOME WITH THE MOON

The home is one of the key areas of lunar influence. It can therefore be especially rewarding to focus on ways to attune your life to the Moon's monthly rhythms. In this section you'll not only discover what your own Moon sign says about the kind of home life you like, but also learn that there are good and not-so-good days for all sorts of domestic tasks. Choose the right day and everything will go like clockwork. Take action on the wrong day and you'll have an uphill struggle to get things done in the way you want.

This part of the book tells you how to make your domestic life run more smoothly with the help of the Moon, whether you're out in the garden or thinking about moving house.

5

The Moon in your home

One of the Moon's astrological realms is our home, because it represents what we find familiar and comforting. So, your moon sign describes where you feel at home and the sort of surroundings that suit you best. The question is, do your current living conditions match your moon?

Natal moon in Aries

There's nothing fussy about your home. It's no-nonsense and practical, because you have far more important things to do than lots of housework. You prefer contemporary furniture to antiques, and you may even shun family heirlooms as being too sentimental. You can't resist the latest technology and labour-saving gadgets, and if you enjoy cooking, you'll have an expensive set of knives that no one else is allowed to use. Wherever you live, it must be big enough so you can entertain your many friends.

Natal moon in Taurus

Taurus is one of the most sensual and tactile signs of the zodiac, so you enjoy living in attractive surroundings, with furnishings that feel good to the touch. Music and art may feature strongly. You prefer traditional furniture to anything wildly contemporary and may have some family items that you treasure. Access to greenery and nature are important for your health, and ideally you should have your own garden or a window box at the very least. Owning your home, rather than renting it, gives you a much-needed sense of security.

Natal moon in Gemini

Given the chance, you go for a home with simple, contemporary furniture and plenty of storage space. You need those cupboards and shelves for storing all the books, magazines, CDs and DVDs you can't resist buying. However, tidying up isn't one of your greatest strengths, so there may be more belongings scattered about on tables than arranged neatly on shelves. There's probably an emphasis on TVs and computers, too, because you love playing around with them. Ideally, you need a home that's big enough to entertain your legion of friends. The duality of Gemini means you may own more than one home, if you can afford it, or may consider someone else's place to be your second home.

Natal moon in Cancer

Home is definitely where the heart is for you. Living in cosy, comfortable, secure and blessedly familiar surroundings is essential to your happiness and given the option, you'll much prefer owning a property than renting it. Even if it's tiny, you lavish plenty of love and care on your home, filling it with cherished memories in the form of keepsakes, photos, paintings, ornaments and maybe even childhood toys and other items that you could never bear to part with. Anyone with a minimalist approach might call it cluttered, but you adore being surrounded by your treasured belongings. Ideally, you need plenty of entertaining space, because you love inviting everyone over to your place and feeding them up.

Natal moon in Leo

Although your moon is in the regal sign of Leo, you don't need to live in a palace. However, you do need a home that you can be proud of because giving a good impression is important to you. You may therefore opt for somewhere small in an expensive area rather than a large home in a less salubrious part of town. You'll fill it with the best things you can afford, and maybe a few items that break your budget but are must-haves nonetheless. Make the most of your creative streak with some clever interior design ideas, and accessorize with lots of photos, paintings (preferably your own work) and other personal touches.

Natal moon in Virgo

You work so hard and spend so much time looking after others that home may end up as merely the place where you sleep (or try to, if you can switch off your busy brain for long enough) rather than where you relax and enjoy being with the rest of the family. Even so, you'll do your best to make your home neat, tidy and spotless, otherwise the perfectionist in you will be bothered by what you consider to be the chaos that surrounds you. More Virgos live alone than those from other signs; and even if you share your home, you definitely need a room of your own that you can retreat to every now and then.

Natal moon in Libra

Home has to be somewhere that's attractive and restful, with friendly neighbours only a stone's throw away. Whether you live in a tiny flat or huge house, there's an emphasis on beautiful objects, lots of books and comfortable furniture, and you prefer toned pastel colours to anything loud or harsh. You enjoy relaxing in a beautiful garden but may draw the line at doing the gardening yourself. Living alone isn't the best option for you, as you need other people around you. If you live with others, you'll do your best to avoid getting caught up in any domestic tension, because it's harmony at all costs as far as you're concerned.

Natal moon in Scorpio

Privacy is an essential part of your life, so your home must offer you a refuge from the rest of the world. It's the place that you retreat to, and you may even regard it as your safe haven. You're very choosy about the people you invite into your home, and generally speaking you prefer to meet them elsewhere. Your home is distinctive and strongly stamped with your unique personality, and you love to surround yourself with books, music and other possessions that have an emotional significance. You're fascinated by old, atmospheric houses – you'd be thrilled to have a ghost in your home, provided it's a friendly one.

Natal moon in Sagittarius

Regardless of where you live and what you live in, there's one essential that you won't compromise on – bookshelves. You adore books and love cramming your home with them even if you've never got round to reading most of them.

Not that you'll admit that! Tidiness doesn't come naturally to you, and you enjoy living in what others might describe as total chaos but you prefer to call a relaxed environment. Your fascination with other cultures and beliefs means you enjoy collecting artworks and artefacts from all round the world, and they're a great talking point for the many friends who enjoy hanging out with you at home.

Natal moon in Capricorn

Less is more, as far as you're concerned. You like a home that's elegant but understated, so you always avoid furnishings that are flashy or fussy. You much prefer antiques to anything highly contemporary and enjoy using items that belonged to your parents or grandparents. Throwing away perfectly good furniture goes against your thrifty instincts, so you may put up with something that you don't like simply because getting rid of it feels like the height of wastefulness. If money permits, you would much rather own your home than rent it; you may even have become a homeowner at a much earlier age than your friends. After all, it makes sound financial sense.

Natal moon in Aquarius

If you share your home with others it's essential for you to have a space you can call your own – preferably a room to retreat to, where your privacy is respected and you can read and think in peace. Living alone may even be your preferred option, with lots of friends to visit you. Ideally, your home should be light and spacious, with plenty of room to breathe. It doesn't have to be expensive or exclusive, but it must have enough space for your books, DVDs, gadgets and collections of eclectic belongings.

Natal moon in Pisces

Like so much in your life, your home must offer you a refuge from the rest of the world. It's your sanctuary, the place where you can escape from problems and difficulties – so you don't invite just anybody to your home. If possible, you'll only invite people you feel a strong connection with and, if you're ultra-sensitive, people who radiate good vibes. You like your home to be comfortable and cosy, with a lived-in atmosphere and lots of possessions that are artistic, esoteric or eclectic – or all three. If it's near water, that's even better.

On the move

Finding and moving into the home of our dreams is exciting but it can also be a stressful business, with possible delays, disappointments and time-wasters to deal with. So, it's important to get the timing right by working with the Moon's monthly cycle.

It isn't always possible to find a day on which every lunar factor is perfect, because sometimes they clash, but always avoid taking action when the Moon is void. At worst, you'll be wasting your time and at best you'll be setting yourself up for delays or disappointments. Also, allow at least a day each side of an eclipse, otherwise the lunar energy will be too strong.

Finding your home sweet home

The time at which you start your search will set the tone for the entire procedure. Follow these rules, which also apply to viewing properties, because the first time you set foot in a possible new home is also important:

- Avoid starting your search or viewing a property when the Moon is void. You may not find anything you like, and if you do and want to go ahead, the subsequent deal will hit delays and snags or might even fall apart.

- Concentrate your search in the period of the waxing Moon, between the new moon and just before the full moon.

- Looking for a home by the sea? Focus on days when the Moon is in Cancer, Scorpio or Pisces.

- Looking for a home in a town? Focus on days when the Moon is in Aries, Gemini or Sagittarius.

- Want to live in the countryside? Choose a day when the Moon is in Taurus, Virgo or Capricorn.

- Want to live high up on a hill or mountain? Look on days when the Moon is in Capricorn or Aquarius.

Negotiating the deal

When you've found your dream home, the next step is to make an offer to buy or rent it at the right moment. Again, timing is everything.

- Negotiations should go well if they're conducted when the Moon is in Aries or Gemini.

- If you want to pay as little as possible, start your negotiations in the Moon's waning period of one day after the full moon and one day before the new moon, and preferably during the disseminating moon phase.

Signing on the dotted line

Getting the timing right when signing a purchase or rental contract is just as important as it is in every other stage of the process.

- Don't sign during a new moon, because you may have overlooked an important clause in the contract.

- If you're buying or renting a home that you'll live in for a long time, sign the contract when the Moon is in a fixed sign – Taurus, Leo or Aquarius.

- If you're buying or renting a home as a temporary measure, sign the contract when the Moon is in Aries, Gemini or Libra.

Moving in

Everything's gone well and you're about to move in. But when should that be? The first step over the threshold of your new home will influence your experience of it in the future, so try to get the timing right.

- Steer clear of a void Moon because, even though the property is now yours, there might be problems or disappointments.

- Ideally, move in during the Moon's first quarter.

- Choose a time when the Moon is in Taurus, Leo, Scorpio or Aquarius for a permanent move, and in Aries, Gemini or Libra for a short stay.

Selling

The timing is just as important here, because if you're selling you no doubt want a successful and smooth sale, and also a good price. Here are the rules about when to put your house up for sale.

- Attract lots of potential buyers by launching your property between the day after a new moon and the day before a full moon.

- Avoid the last quarter and balsamic phases because people may be difficult to deal with.

- Choose a day when the Moon is in Taurus, Cancer, Scorpio or Capricorn.

The happy household

The Moon is the planet that governs all things to do with the home, so it's a great guide to the most effective ways of looking after your domestic world.

Cleaning

If you were born with the Moon in Virgo, you may not need any lunar help with cleaning because you're probably already best friends with your vacuum cleaner. Otherwise, these hints could help.

- If you're planning a short burst of cleaning, time it for just after the new moon, when you'll have plenty of energy.

- If you're planning a thorough cleaning session, do it during a last quarter or balsamic moon because your efforts will be more effective and long-lasting.

- Avoid days when the Moon is in Taurus, Leo or Libra because you'll soon run out of steam and want to do something else.

- Choose a day when the Moon is in Virgo, Capricorn or Aquarius, when you'll do the job properly.

- Clean windows and mirrors on days when the Moon is waning in Aries, Gemini, Leo, Libra, Sagittarius or Aquarius. You'll have fewer streaks.

- Choose a day when the Moon is in Cancer, Scorpio or Pisces for cleaning jobs that will need a lot of water and elbow grease.

Decluttering

It can be very easy to accumulate clutter, especially if you were born with the Moon in Cancer, which loves to be surrounded by familiar and nostalgic objects.

- Start the decluttering in the period between the start of the last quarter moon and the end of the balsamic moon.

- If you want to go through each piece of clutter carefully, choose a day when the Moon is in Taurus, Leo, Virgo, Scorpio or Capricorn.

- If you want to get rid of lots of things without being sidetracked by looking at them, choose a day when the Moon is in Aries or Sagittarius.

- Avoid the Moon in Gemini or you'll invent an excuse to down tools at the first sign of boredom.

- Avoid the Moon in Cancer in case you decide to keep everything because you can't bear to get rid of it!

Repairs

The Moon tells us the best time to carry out repairs to our belongings.

- Choose a day when the Moon is waning, and preferably between the last quarter and balsamic moons.

- Tackle repairs to electrical or technological goods when the Moon is in Aquarius.

- Carry out simple running repairs when the Moon is in Capricorn.

- Do fiddly or very detailed repairs when the Moon is in Virgo.

- Avoid days when the Moon is in Aries because you could get easily bored.

- Avoid days when the Moon is in Sagittarius because whoever does the repairs may be clumsy or in a hurry.

- Repairs to cars, bicycles and motorbikes are best done when the Moon is in Gemini.

Decorating

This can be a fiddly and time-consuming process, so it makes sense to choose a time that's favourable for the Moon. The general guidelines below apply whether you're decorating the inside or outside of your home.

- Do any painting, gluing or varnishing when the Moon is waning, so choose a suitable day between the full and new moons. This reduces your chances of inhaling harmful vapours released by the products you're using.

- Avoid days when the Moon is in one of the Water signs (Cancer, Scorpio and Pisces) because it will take longer than usual for paints, varnishes and other products to dry.

- Avoid days when the Moon is in Leo because the products will dry too quickly and could flake.

- Plan an interior design scheme or browse soft furnishings when the Moon is in Taurus, Cancer, Leo or Libra, and also preferably when it's waxing.

- Begin decorating a child's bedroom when the Moon is in Gemini.

- Begin decorating a couple's bedroom when the Moon is in Libra.

- Prepare to decorate a kitchen or dining room when the Moon is in Cancer, but don't paint or varnish it.

- Begin decorating a sitting room when the Moon is in Leo.

- Begin decorating a bathroom when the Moon is in Virgo.

Gardening by the Moon

Do you ever dream of having a garden that truly flourishes, with flowers that bloom freely, vegetables that are juicy and delicious, and shrubs that look healthy and happy? If so, lunar gardening could be the answer.

No, this doesn't mean getting out your fork and spade only when the Moon is shining brightly in the sky! Instead, it involves planning your gardening schedule according to the path of the Moon through the zodiac each month. This is quite simple and can be very effective, as you'll discover if you try it yourself. Your plants will grow better, more healthily and will be more resistant to pests and diseases than plants grown conventionally.

There are some basic rules that can sound rather complex at first; but once you get the hang of them, you'll find they quickly become second nature. In lunar gardening you track three important factors:

- the sign of the Moon in the sidereal zodiac on any given day

- the element that governs the sign occupied by the Moon on that day

- whether the Moon is ascending or descending

The sidereal zodiac

If you would like to try lunar gardening, don't simply look up the sign of the Moon for a particular day online or in an ordinary almanac or planetary table (also known as an ephemeris). You need that information for every other part of the book but not this one! Lunar gardening tracks the 27.3-day sidereal path of the Moon, which is its journey around the zodiac in relation to the constellations, and ignores the 29.53-day synodic path, which consists of one complete cycle of the Moon's phases, such as from one new moon to the next.

The sidereal Moon lags 24° behind the synodic Moon. Each sign of the zodiac consists of 30°, which means that the sidereal Moon is almost one sign behind the synodic Moon. A rough way of working out the sidereal path of the Moon is to look up the synodic position of the Moon on any given day and then mentally shift it backwards to the previous sign. For instance, when, using the synodic calendar, the Moon is in Aquarius, it will be in Capricorn, using the sidereal calendar, unless it's right at the start or end of the sign. This is a simple way of converting the Moon from its synodic sign to its sidereal sign, especially if you're just starting to experiment with lunar gardening. However, if you wish to be more precise, you can buy books and apps that will give you all the relevant information for lunar gardening for each day of the coming year.

Elements

As explained earlier in the book (see pages 30–53), each sign of the zodiac belongs to a particular element – Air, Earth, Fire or Water. The theory of lunar gardening is that as the Moon moves through each sign, it transmits the energy of that element to the Earth. Each element governs a specific type of plant, as you can see from the table on page 122. To understand which plants belong to which category, you need to think about your main reason for growing them. For instance, all plants have leaves and the Water element relates to leaves, but that doesn't mean that all plants are governed by the Water element. Instead, Water governs all plants that are grown solely for their leaves, such as lettuces. You can read much more about the elements on pages 122–5.

The ascending and descending Moon

Here's the final essential piece of the lunar gardening jigsaw puzzle. As the Moon moves around the zodiac each month it's either ascending or descending. When ascending in the northern hemisphere it's moving between the start of the constellation of Sagittarius and the end of Taurus, and it descends between the start of Gemini and the end of Scorpio. The reverse is true in the southern hemisphere.

Please note that this cycle of the Moon has nothing to do with the waxing and waning cycle of new and full moons, and they shouldn't be confused.

The sidereal path of the Moon

This is the path the Moon takes as it travels across the backdrop of the constellations. It takes 27.3 days to complete its journey from the start of Aries to the end of Pisces.

Elementary gardening

Once you begin to garden using the four elements as your guide to what to do and when, you'll find that the system works really well. The results will soon speak for themselves, such as seeds that germinate strongly and develop into sturdy seedlings, and fruit and vegetable crops that taste good and, where appropriate, are deliciously juicy.

The rules of lunar gardening are very simple. Whether you're digging the soil, sowing seeds, transplanting seedlings, weeding, hoeing, pruning or carrying out any other sort of cultivation, you always do it when the Moon is in the appropriate element for the type of plant you are working with.

The elements and types of plant

The rules about which types of plant belong to which element are simple and easy to remember, although there are a few cases when these are open to interpretation, as you'll soon discover. The table below shows which plants relate to which element and which signs.

ELEMENT	SIGNS	TYPE OF PLANT
Fire	Aries, Leo, Sagittarius	Fruit- or seed-bearing
Earth	Taurus, Virgo, Capricorn	Roots and bulbs
Air	Gemini, Libra, Aquarius	Flower-bearing
Water	Cancer, Scorpio, Pisces	Leafy

Although the vast majority of plants fall neatly into a particular element, a few need a little thinking about. For instance, there aren't many vegetables in the Air element because this rules flower-bearing plants. How can a vegetable also be a flower? If you have ever seen broccoli spears that are past their best, you may have noticed that they have started to turn yellow. If you look closer, you'll realize that you're looking at tiny yellow flowers. That's because the curly tops of broccoli are actually flower buds, but we don't realize this because we usually eat them long before they burst into bloom. Cauliflowers are classified as a Water crop by some lunar gardeners and as an Air crop by others; so if you want to grow them perhaps you should experiment and see which element works best for you in your garden.

The descriptions that follow will give you a good idea of which plants belong to which element. Most of the plants listed are edible, but the rules of lunar gardening apply to non-edible plants as well. Whenever you're trying to decide which element is the correct one, remember that this system focuses on your reason for growing the plant and not necessarily on its physical shape. For instance, if you buy a bag of daffodil bulbs because you want your garden to be full of their flowers the following spring, you might at first think that they belong to the Earth element because they're bulbs. However, you're growing them for their flowers, so they fall into the Air element instead.

Fire plants
These are plants grown for their fruits or seeds. They include soft fruits (such as raspberries and strawberries), stone fruits

(such as cherries and apricots) and top fruits (such as apples and pears), as well as tomatoes, cucumbers, chillies, squashes, peppers and beans. They also include ornamental shrubs grown for their attractive berries (which are inedible, of course, unless you happen to be a bird), such as pyracantha.

Earth plants
These are plants grown for their roots, and they include carrots, parsnips, potatoes, radishes, onions, garlic, turmeric and ginger.

Air plants
Here we have plants grown for their flowers, such as geraniums, violets and roses. Flowering bulbs and rhizomes, such as tulips and dahlias, also belong here because they're grown for their flowers, not their bulbs. In the vegetable kingdom, Air plants include broccoli and artichokes, because their heads are flower buds. Flowers grown specifically to be eaten, such as nasturtiums and calendula, also belong here.

Water plants
These are all plants grown for their leaves, and include leafy herbs, cabbages, leeks, lettuces, cress and chard. Although you might imagine that cauliflowers belong to the Air element, some lunar gardeners consider them to be leaf plants and therefore members of the Water element instead.

Fine-tuning
The ideal method of lunar gardening is to only work on plants that belong to a particular element, or the soil in which the plants will be grown, when the Moon is in

that element. In other words, even if you're merely tidying up your greenhouse in readiness for planting out tomato seedlings, you should do that on a Fire day.

If it isn't convenient to garden on the appropriate day, it's perfectly acceptable to choose a day when the Moon is in the element either side of the ideal one. The element that must be avoided is the one that's opposite the ideal element. For example, if you need to transplant some flower seedlings and can't wait for the appropriate Air day, you can work on them on an Earth or Water day instead. However, you must avoid cultivating them on a Fire day, because this is the opposite element.

You must also avoid doing any gardening at all at least six hours either side of a new or full moon, and at least twelve hours either side of an eclipse. This is because the energy of the Moon is too strong and may adversely affect the plants as well as the soil.

The rise and fall of the Moon

The other consideration is whether the Moon is in its ascending or descending phase. When the Moon is in its ascending cycle, a plant's sap rises into its leaves, flowers and fruit, so it's a good time to sow seeds and also to cut off the tips of plants that you want to graft onto another plant.

When the Moon is in its descending cycle, a plant's sap is also descending. Therefore, this is the time to do work that involves the plant's root system, such as planting seedlings, thinning them out and propagating plants by dividing or layering them.

Putting the elements and Moon cycle together

By combining the element of a day in question with the phase of the Moon cycle, you'll know exactly which jobs to carry out in the garden. For example, an Earth day when the Moon is ascending is good for sowing the seeds of root crops but shouldn't be used for any activities connected with Water plants (the opposite element to Earth), and an Air day when the Moon is descending is good for transplanting flower seedlings but not for doing anything connected to plants associated with Fire (the opposite element to Air).

Harvesting and storing

The Moon's effects on plants, and on the action of their sap (plants have more sap during the ascending lunar phase and are drier during the descending lunar phase), means that it's important to follow the rules of lunar gardening when harvesting, storing or preserving crops. This helps to reduce possible spoilage, such as when you want to know the right time to let a crop of onions dry naturally without rotting, or when to make jars of jam ready for the winter. With a little forethought and planning, you can use the Moon's cycles and signs to help you choose the best time to harvest and store food. When harvesting and storing produce, you must follow the sidereal calendar that's used in lunar gardening (see page 173).

It's elementary

Here's a quick reminder of which element governs which type of plant.

FIRE	Plants bearing fruits or seeds
EARTH	Plants grown for their roots or bulbs
AIR	Plants grown for their flowers
WATER	Plants grown for their leaves

Harvesting

Although it might seem logical that the best time to harvest food crops is during their relevant phase of the Moon, this isn't always true.

- Unless you will be eating a plant immediately, avoid harvesting it on a day when the Moon is void.

- The best time to harvest Fire element plants is on Fire days, preferably when the Moon is ascending (so in Aries or Sagittarius in the northern hemisphere). Avoid harvesting plants on Air days.

- The best time to harvest root plants is on Earth days. Avoid harvesting them on Water days.

- The best time to harvest Air element plants is on Air days. Avoid harvesting them on Fire days.

- Avoid harvesting Water element plants on Water or Earth days. They'll taste and keep better if you harvest them on Fire or Air days. Very wet Water plants, such as lettuce, are best picked when the Moon is waning, and first thing in the morning, before the dew on them has dried.

Storing

After all your hard work growing fruit, vegetables and herbs, it's essential to store them at the right time so they'll stay in good condition for as long as possible. The Moon's influence regulates the amount of moisture in the plants; storing them at the wrong time can mean they're either too dry when you eat them or too wet when you store them, so they soon start to rot. Of course, you must ensure that the crops are in perfect condition, because even the correct lunar phase won't prevent a damaged fruit or vegetable rotting in storage and affecting the rest of the crop.

- Store Fire element plants when the Moon is waning in one of the Fire or Air signs, so they aren't too juicy.

- Store Earth element plants when the Moon is in one of the Earth signs. Avoid storing them on days when the Moon is in one of the Water signs.

- If you're planning to store plants such as herbs and onions in their dried state, do so when the Moon is waning while in the appropriate element.

Preserving fruits and vegetables

There are lots of ways to preserve foods, including making jams, jellies, pickles and chutneys.

- Make jam or marmalade when the Moon is waxing and in one of the Water signs – Cancer, Scorpio or Pisces. The watery nature of these days will ensure the preserves are juicy. However, it may take longer than normal to get the jam or marmalade to the correct setting point, so be patient.

- Chutneys and pickles are often made from a combination of fruit and vegetables. Make them on days when the Moon is waxing in one of the Water signs – Cancer, Scorpio or Pisces.

At home with the Moon:

MONTHLY DOS AND DON'TS AT A GLANCE

MOON IN ARIES DAYS

DO

★ put plenty of elbow grease into jobs you do around the house

★ stay active to avoid a build-up of nervous energy

★ try some adventurous cooking

★ tinker with an engine to get it working

★ get busy with some DIY, but only if you know what you're doing

DON'T

☆ get impatient when a task doesn't go as well as you'd like

☆ make spur-of-the-moment domestic decisions without consulting the rest of the household first

☆ be in such a hurry while cooking that you burn or scald yourself

MOON IN TAURUS DAYS

DO

★ consider changing or brightening up some of the soft furnishings at home

★ work on your garden by digging the vegetable patch

★ relax and do as little as possible

★ buy some flowers for your home

DON'T

☆ get stuck in a domestic rut

☆ insist on following a tradition for no good reason

☆ even consider making a radical decision

☆ be possessive of loved ones

MOON IN GEMINI DAYS

DO

★ invite some friends over on the spur of the moment

★ change the furniture around

★ tidy up your collection of books or DVDs

★ recycle old magazines and newspapers

★ buy a new labour-saving gadget

DON'T

☆ leave a trail of discarded items everywhere you go

☆ get distracted and forget to put out the bins

☆ start one household job before finishing the previous one

☆ say the wrong thing to a neighbour or sibling

MOON IN CANCER DAYS

DO

★ enjoy your home comforts as much as possible

★ look through old photos and other keepsakes

★ throw a big family get-together

★ cherish your favourite belongings by taking care of them

★ turn out your attic or storage cupboard to see what's there

DON'T

☆ hold on to possessions you no longer need

☆ get upset if someone can't visit you

☆ regard a family member or pet as your personal property

☆ think that you can't get rid of something because it once belonged to a loved one

MOON IN LEO DAYS

DO

★ eat your food off your best china, even if you're only having a sandwich

★ bask in the sunshine

★ plant sun-loving flowers or herbs

★ suggest drawing up a housework rota so everyone can do their bit

★ refresh your home with a new piece of artwork

DON'T

☆ mix with anyone who's a property snob

☆ issue orders to the rest of the household

☆ compare your home with someone else's, whether favourably or unfavourably

☆ turn your pet into an extension of yourself

MOON IN VIRGO DAYS

DO

★ give your kitchen and bathroom a spring clean

★ get rid of any food that's past its best

★ make running repairs to your clothes and belongings

★ clean and tidy your pet's bedding

★ wash your hairbrushes and combs

DON'T

☆ vacuum the carpets into threadbare extinction

☆ fret over all the little problems with your home

☆ tell yourself you're lazy if you don't do ten different things at once

☆ forget the benefits of taking life gently

MOON IN LIBRA DAYS

DO

★ scent your home with candles or bowls of potpourri

★ play your favourite pieces of music

★ buy yourself some flowers

★ relax on the sofa and do absolutely nothing

★ sleep on freshly laundered and ironed sheets

DON'T

☆ think there's something wrong with you if you live alone

☆ feel you have to keep the peace at home when you really need to let off steam

☆ feel bereft if you've got to spend time on your own

☆ be too emotionally dependent on your pet

MOON IN SCORPIO DAYS

DO

★ release emotional tension by doing the housework or gardening

★ burn bunches of dried sage (known as 'smudging') or use crystals to release trapped energy in your home

★ open all the windows and let in the fresh air

★ relax in the garden while reading a thriller or doing a puzzle

DON'T

☆ throw out something precious in a fit of pique

☆ cut off your nose to spite your face

☆ be reluctant to do things differently at home

☆ invite someone out of politeness when you're longing to be by yourself

MOON IN SAGITTARIUS DAYS

DO

★ have a great big tidy-up

★ organize your travel memorabilia

★ go through your book collection and give away duplicate copies

★ buy an exotic plant for your home or the garden

★ invite some friends over

DON'T

☆ take any risks when handling delicate china or glassware

☆ leave your pet to fend for itself for too long while you're out and about

☆ forget to renew your passport or any other travel passes or rail cards

MOON IN CAPRICORN DAYS

DO

★ make yourself sit down and unwind

★ polish your wooden furniture

★ consult an architect for advice about renovating your home

★ defrost the fridge and freezer

★ look after your antique possessions

DON'T

☆ forget to protect delicate plants in frosty or snowy weather

☆ think the cost of something is more important than the comfort it will bring

☆ use cleaning products that you know will irritate your skin

☆ worry that your home isn't smart or expensive enough

MOON IN AQUARIUS DAYS

DO

★ tidy up your desk or working area at home

★ clean your computer or tablet

★ change the look of a room by moving the furniture around

★ encourage family members to have an interesting discussion

★ do your own thing at home

DON'T

☆ be so contrary that you upset someone

☆ neglect your need to be your own person in order to fit in with others

☆ spend too much time in front of a screen

☆ forget to get some fresh air and exercise

MOON IN PISCES DAYS

DO

★ put your favourite essential oil in a diffuser

★ check your carpets for moth holes and other damage

★ clean out the dust from the hidden corners of your rooms

★ burn some incense or a scented candle

★ create a mini altar in a private area of a room

DON'T

☆ feel defeated by that mountain of washing up or laundry

☆ forget the importance of snuggling under the bedclothes with a favourite book

☆ neglect your sleep

☆ be manipulated by a family member

HEALTH, BEAUTY AND WELLBEING

Make the most of lunar timing by planning your health and beauty regimes around the Moon's phases and signs. You'll discover the best times to relax each month and recharge your batteries, as well as the days on which you can enjoy being active and busy. This will help you to plan ahead and avoid cramming too many activities into those days when you need to take life gently. You'll also learn what your natal moon sign says about the sort of food you like to eat, especially when you're looking for some emotional comfort.

If you want to know when the best time is to get your hair cut or to give yourself a beauty treatment, this section of the book will give you the answers and help you to get the most out of all your efforts.

In the rhythm

Our bodies are governed by many different rhythms. The ones that most of us have heard of are the circadian rhythms, which dictate our waking and sleeping times and run for roughly 24 hours. These are the rhythms that make us feel sleepy at night and wide awake in the morning, although our modern way of living, and especially the increased use of blue light in computers and other gadgets, means that our circadian rhythms are often disturbed. This can lead to many ailments, from a generalized sense of fatigue because we aren't getting enough sleep to more serious problems, such as obesity and diabetes.

Larks and night owls

Some of us are naturally alert first thing in the morning, leaping out of bed and throwing back the curtains. We start to flag in the evenings, though, as we start to feel sleepy. By contrast, some of us are slow starters in the morning, preferring to pull the duvet over our heads and hit the snooze button on the alarm, and then fire on all cylinders late at night.

Why is this? You might imagine it's just the luck of the draw and caused by personal preference, yet it seems that the time when we were born could have a huge influence over whether we're larks or night owls. Psychologists working at Cleveland State University in Ohio, United States, in 2010 tested the mental performance levels of students in the mornings and again in the late afternoons, and then compared the results with the times of day when the students were born. They discovered that the students born in the morning scored better in the morning tests, while those born later in the day did better in the late-afternoon tests. Perhaps our circadian rhythms are activated when we're born and see bright lights for the first time after months in the darkness of our mother's womb.

The Moon and the heart

It seems that it's not only astrologers who are fascinated by the rhythms of
the Moon. In 2013, researchers at Rhode Island Hospital in the United
States studied the correlation between certain forms of cardiac surgery
and the phases of the Moon. They discovered that the chances of dying
after repair to an aortic dissection (injury to the aorta) were reduced if the
procedure was performed during the waning full moon. What's more, the
length of stay of the patients was reduced from an average of fourteen
days to ten days if they had the repair during the full moon.

The Moon and the stomach

The cardiac research is particularly fascinating because, generally
speaking, we bleed more, not less, at a full moon. A study conducted in
2004 in a hospital in Barcelona, Spain, found that this was true because
there were more admissions for patients (especially male patients) with
gastrointestinal bleeding during the full moon phase. There was, though, a
considerable variation in the number of patients admitted with
gastrointestinal bleeding throughout the lunar cycle, so more studies
would be needed to clarify the Moon's influence.

The Moon and you

The medical research mentioned above focuses on very specific ailments
rather than general conditions. However, you can conduct your own
research into the effect of the Moon's phases and cycles by noting how
you feel at different times of the month. Try to do this as objectively as
possible, perhaps by recording in a daily journal your physical, mental and
emotional states, as well as your sleep patterns, but without taking
conscious note of the Moon's signs or phases. At the end of your
experiment, you can look through the results to see if there are any
correlations between your moods, physical and mental health and sleep,
and the signs and phases of the Moon. The results could surprise you!

Your moon sign and food

The Moon represents food, as well as other aspects of life that feed us, such as the things that feel familiar and nurture us emotionally. So the sign of your moon describes what you like to eat, and how you like to eat it. Consult the Moon signs of your family and friends to discover whether their needs differ from yours.

 Natal moon in Aries In common with so many things in your life, you don't like waiting around for food. You don't waste time when you're eating it, either. You love fast food – food that's ready quickly and that you can consume at breakneck speed. Yes, you enjoy a leisurely meal with friends or family, where the conversation is as important as the food, but even then, you'll have finished eating long before everyone else. You enjoy all sorts of cuisines but have a penchant for hot and spicy food – the more chillies, the better.

Natal moon in Taurus Ah, food! It's one of your greatest solaces in life, so you pay lots of attention to it. You enjoy cooking meals from scratch, partly for the sensual experience and partly because you like to know what you're eating. You're suspicious of food that's been mucked about with until it's unrecognizable. Puddings and cakes, and simple dishes involving potatoes or pasta, make you happy; and chocolate is your best friend. When life gets tough, you find comfort in food, sometimes to the detriment of your waistline – at which point it's just as important for you to consider why you eat as what you eat.

Natal moon in Gemini A little bit of this and a small slice of that is the way you prefer to eat, rather than a huge plate of just one thing. Variety is essential for you, so if you enjoy cooking, you'll want to keep experimenting with different cuisines and ingredients. You adore sociable meals, because you consider the conversation to be as important as the food; but if you're on your own you're quite happy to eat while reading, watching TV or scrolling through social media sites. Your busy life means you often eat on the hoof, and there may be times when you exist more on sandwiches and snacks than on proper meals.

Natal moon in Cancer Food and happiness go together for you. Eating something delicious soothes you when times are tough and makes you happy when there's something to celebrate. It brings you together with loved ones as often as possible, because you adore cooking mammoth meals and feeding everyone until they beg for mercy. You'd much rather cook family favourites and trusted recipes than experiment with unusual ingredients or new styles of cooking. You're very sensitive emotionally, and if you can't find any other outlet for your damaged feelings you may resort to comfort eating to help you to swallow your pain.

Natal moon in Leo This is the sign of a real foodie. Your leonine moon makes you appreciate quality rather than quantity, and you can't resist a few delicious luxuries every now and then. You may even buy some items, such as attractive tins or decorative bottles, to put on display, rather than consume, because you love the way they look. Cooking is something you enjoy, but only on your own terms. Given the choice, you'd much prefer to spend hours creating a celebratory and sociable feast for loved ones than dash around each day throwing together an everyday meal that everyone eats while watching TV or looking at their phones. Your culinary talents need more appreciation than that!

Natal moon in Virgo The sign of Virgo shows a deep interest in health and nutrition, so you know exactly what you should eat even if you sometimes fail to put that knowledge into practice – something that can spark a strong sense of guilt. You're also aware of the foods and drinks that don't agree with you and will avoid them at all costs. There are bound to be one or two things to avoid, because you have quite a sensitive digestive system, which becomes even more touchy whenever you get anxious or work too hard. You might find that consciously relaxing makes a huge difference to your gut.

Natal moon in Libra Food is one of the great pleasures of your life, especially if you can share it with people you love. You adore eating out, particularly in up-market restaurants, or having a romantic dinner à *deux*, but you also enjoy cooking at home. Mind you, even if you're only making some quick beans on toast, you'll take care to present the food attractively, putting it on an elegant plate or setting a place at the table. It's highly likely that you have a sweet tooth, with almost zero resistance to chocolate or creamy foods. But even if sugary things don't appeal, you may still have battles with your weight, especially as you get older. After all, Libra is the sign of the scales!

Natal moon in Scorpio Food can be a bit of a conundrum to you. You love eating it and can gain great solace from it when you're going through a difficult time, especially if you tend to bottle up your feelings and keep them to yourself. However, you're often concerned about gaining weight or eating the wrong things – two ideas that may have been fostered in you as a child. Strong flavours really appeal to you, rather than anything too bland, so you may enjoy such foods as game, hot curries and richly spiced Middle Eastern dishes. You don't care for very sweet foods, although it's a different story when it comes to dark chocolate.

Natal moon in Sagittarius There's no doubt that you enjoy eating, but it's the social aspects of food that appeal most of all. Whether you've done the cooking yourself or you're eating out, you love long leisurely meals with friends and family, in which you all catch up on each other's news and put the world to rights. However, if you're on your own you may not bother to cook a proper meal and will make do with a quick snack, concocted from whatever you happen to find in the fridge – which can lead to some inventive combinations. With your love of travel and fascination with other cultures, it's no surprise that you enjoy a wide range of foods from all over the world.

Natal moon in Capricorn While those from some moon signs like to eat until they're full, and then squeeze in a little bit more, it's a different story for you. That's because you tend to be quite strict with yourself, and may even investigate an eating regime, such as a type of fasting, that limits the amount of food you have each day. Even if you do eat whatever you want, you're unlikely to overdo it. This is probably because of the way you were brought up – don't eat too much, and don't be wasteful by not eating what you're given. Capricorn has a strong affinity with time, so you may eat at set times, rather than grazing all day or grabbing something whenever you're hungry.

Natal moon in Aquarius As far as you're concerned, it's the social aspects of food that mean most to you. Chatting with friends or family over a long lunch or dinner gives you the best of both worlds. When you're on your own, you may not be particularly interested in making a proper meal for yourself, so you regard food as fuel rather than fun. However, you're concerned about the ethics involved in the food you eat and may even have strict rules about eating a mainly organic, vegetarian or vegan diet. If you feel very strongly about this, you won't be able to keep your thoughts to yourself.

Natal moon in Pisces Sometimes you like eating simply because it's a good way of blocking out difficult emotions, but you should take care not to overdo it. At other times, you may find that you can't eat anything because you feel so churned up or upset that your stomach simply can't cope. Either way, it means that your feelings can be closely connected with your eating habits. Because this is such a sensitive placing for the Moon, you may have an allergy or intolerance to some foods or drinks, and others may be best avoided because they tend to make you feel sluggish or slightly weird.

The Moon and relaxation

We all need to relax every now and then, so we can balance our exertions and stresses. However, it's not always easy to unwind, because some lunar phases and signs make us feel energetic or tense. Here's your guide to going with the lunar flow, according to the Moon's sign on any given day.

Generally speaking, we always feel more energetic and buzzier in the first two weeks of the Moon's cycle, between the new and full moons. That's because our energy is waxing, just like the Moon's light. The full moon itself can be a time of tension, because things are coming to fruition, so there's a lot to do. Once the Moon begins to wane, however, we become more relaxed, depending on the Moon's sign, in readiness for the start of the next lunar cycle.

Moon in Aries days You feel buzzy and alert, finding it hard to switch off. Impatience and restlessness may interrupt your sleep, so try to burn off all of your nervous energy in positive ways during the day.

Moon in Taurus days Calm and placid, you may struggle to motivate yourself at times. You enjoy taking life easy and doing as little as possible. This is one of the most sensual times of the month, so enjoy it.

Moon in Gemini days It's a day when you feel wired and possibly even jumpy. Avoid stimulants, such as coffee and fizzy drinks, and don't burn the candle at both ends. Flicking through a magazine or watching a TV programme helps you to unwind.

Moon in Cancer days You need your home comforts, even to the point of feeling wound up when you're away from everything and everyone that you hold dear. Relaxing on the sofa, snoozing in a deck chair or having a cosy lie-in appeals to you right now.

Moon in Leo days Relax by doing something that brings out your creative streak, particularly dancing or painting. You'll be able to lose yourself in it, shutting off distracting thoughts or worries. Being playful or sporty helps you to unwind, too.

Moon in Virgo days Relaxing isn't easy right now because you're conscious of all the things you think you should be doing instead. Beware of letting duty call the shots. Practise mindfulness or meditation to calm down your racing thoughts.

Moon in Libra days Listening to a favourite piece of music or being with a special person helps you to unwind. You'll also try to avoid any rows. This is a good day for slowing down your normal pace of life, and you may feel sleepier than usual.

Moon in Scorpio days Life feels rather intense, which makes you anxious about what might be round the corner. You'll feel better if you can confide about what's troubling you, either to a trusted friend or in your private journal.

Moon in Sagittarius days You aren't in the mood for a complete rest because there are so many things you want to do. Losing yourself in a good book will help you to unwind, as will going for a walk or visiting somewhere with a cultural emphasis.

Moon in Capricorn days It's hard to relax because your responsibilities are weighing heavily on you. Which is why you need to unwind – right now. Get together with someone who makes you laugh and reminds you of the good things in life.

Moon in Aquarius days You'll feel good if you can be spontaneous, because having to abide by a strict routine will make you feel trapped and frustrated. Getting involved in a relaxing pastime or hobby will take you into another realm.

Moon in Pisces days You're looking for a means of escape from any difficulties you're currently facing – but go easy on the alcohol. A warm and scented bath will make you unwind, as will a swim in the sea, a walk by a stretch of river or some meditation.

Healthy living

Do you want to eat more healthily, give up something that you know is bad for you or start to slim down? Are you keen to increase the amount of exercise you take each day? The Moon governs food and also our habits, so working with the monthly lunar energies will help you to achieve your aim. You still need willpower, but the Moon can help you with that. Make sure the Moon isn't void when starting any health improvements, so there are fewer chances of setbacks or disappointments.

Improving your diet

This is a work in progress for most of us, but here are some helpful pointers for when to add good things to what you eat.

- Make a conscious decision to add healthy foods to your diet on days when the Moon is in Virgo or Scorpio.

- Start eating more fresh vegetables, fruit and herbs when the Moon is in one of the Earth signs – Taurus, Virgo or Capricorn.

- Start eating more fish when the Moon is in one of the Water signs – Cancer, Scorpio or Pisces.

- Start eating more spices when the Moon is one of the Fire signs – Aries, Leo or Sagittarius.

- Boost your willpower by starting your regime at the first quarter moon, when you're full of determination.

Slimming down

If there's more of you than you'd like, you can use the power of the Moon's phases and signs to strengthen your resolve and set you on the right path.

- Begin your weight-loss regime during the waning phase of the Moon, and never during the waxing phase.

- Start when the Moon is in Aries, Gemini, Leo, Virgo, Capricorn or Aquarius.

Putting on weight

Not everyone battles with trying to lose weight. Some of us struggle to gain it, especially after a period of tension or illness.

- Start when the Moon is in its waxing phase, and especially during the crescent or first quarter phases.

- Begin your new regime when the Moon is in Taurus, Cancer, Leo or Libra.

Willpower

Yes, you can do this! That's what you have to remember, and choosing the right time to start your new health regime will help you to stick with it.

- Start your regime during the waxing lunar phase if you want to give yourself a boost, such as having more energy or eating better.

- Start your regime during the waning lunar phase if you're aiming to lose weight or want to kick an unhelpful habit.

- If you intend to lose weight, be extra vigilant when the Moon is in Taurus, Cancer, Leo and Libra, because these are days when your willpower is low and you're easily tempted by treats that are on the banned list.

Getting more exercise

Yes, the Moon can assist you here, too. So let those lunar rhythms help you start off on the right foot – pun intended.

- Make sure the start of your regime of increased activity coincides with the waxing Moon.

- Try to match the type of exercise with the sign that the Moon occupies on any given day.

- Go swimming, do aquarobics or any other water-based exercise on days when the Moon is in a Water sign – Cancer, Scorpio or Pisces.

- Go running or jogging on days when the Moon is in Aries, Gemini or Sagittarius.

- Do any exercise that requires muscular strength, such as lifting weights, when the Moon is in Aries or Scorpio.

- Go to a dance class when the Moon is in Virgo or Pisces.

- Go to a yoga class when the Moon is in Aries, Aquarius or Pisces.

Meditation and mindfulness

Want to introduce a sense of peace into your busy life? Let the Moon guide you in the right direction.

- If you're really stressed or anxious, start when the Moon is waning.

- If you want to do this more out of curiosity than need, start when the Moon is waxing.

- Time the first session for when the Moon is in a peaceful and contemplative sign – Taurus, Libra or Pisces.

The body beautiful:
MONTHLY DOS AND DON'TS AT A GLANCE

MOON IN ARIES DAYS

DO

★ take exercise that builds muscle and core strength

★ have gentle treatments on your face

★ eat spicy food if it agrees with you

★ get off the sofa and keep as active as possible

DON'T

☆ have any surgical interventions on your face or head

☆ overexercise to the point of straining your muscles or joints

☆ take risks when driving

☆ spend too long in the sun

MOON IN TAURUS DAYS

DO

★ have gentle treatments on your throat or neck

★ sing – it will make you happy

★ enjoy an aromatherapy massage or treatment

★ get into the fresh air

★ indulge your senses

DON'T

☆ have any surgical interventions on your throat or neck

☆ eat too much food, especially if it's very rich

☆ spend too much time being sedentary

☆ get bogged down in the same old routine until your energy starts to drain away

MOON IN GEMINI DAYS

DO

★ keep active so you can burn off excess nervous energy – but don't overdo it

★ immerse yourself in a book

★ ride a bike or go skateboarding

★ record your thoughts and feelings in a journal

★ give yourself a manicure or get your nails done

DON'T

☆ burn the candle at both ends

☆ have any surgical interventions on your arms, hands or lungs

☆ skip meals or exist on coffee and sugary snacks

☆ trip over something because you're in too much of a hurry to get things done

MOON IN CANCER DAYS

DO

★ go for a swim in the sea or a walk along the beach

★ paint with watercolours

★ soak in a scented bath

★ buy some probiotics or vitamin pills

★ smother your body in a hydrating cream or oil

DON'T

☆ have any surgical interventions on your breasts or stomach

☆ eat too much dairy food

☆ feel overwhelmed by painful memories

☆ be tempted by food or drink that can upset your stomach

MOON IN LEO DAYS

DO

★ give yourself a luxurious treat

★ express yourself creatively or artistically

★ spend time with some of your favourite people

★ have a session of gentle cardio exercise

★ try some stretching exercises

DON'T

☆ lift heavy objects and damage your back

☆ have any surgical interventions on your spine or heart

☆ leave the house without looking your best

☆ sit hunched over your desk

MOON IN VIRGO DAYS

DO

★ enjoy feeling in control of what you're doing

★ find ways to relax if you start to feel stressed

★ eat plenty of healthy food and drink lots of water

★ take a yoga or Pilates class

★ start a new eating regime

DON'T

☆ have any surgical interventions on your digestive system

☆ curl up with a health magazine and then worry that you have every ailment you read about

☆ start to fret about minor problems until you can't think about anything else

☆ tell yourself you don't have time for a proper lunch hour

MOON IN LIBRA DAYS

DO

★ relax by listening to some favourite music

★ ensure you're drinking plenty of liquids

★ give yourself a beautifying treatment

★ wear a flattering outfit

DON'T

☆ have any surgical interventions on your kidneys

☆ drink too much alcohol

☆ spend too long in an untidy room

☆ forget to stop and smell the flowers

MOON IN SCORPIO DAYS

DO

★ get some enjoyable exercise

★ have an aromatherapy massage using frankincense or another deep-acting oil

★ start keeping a record of your dreams

★ try some dry-skin brushing

DON'T

☆ have any surgical interventions on your reproductive system

☆ let yourself be dragged down by negative emotions

☆ try to go to sleep immediately after a row

☆ sit in a stuffy atmosphere for too long

MOON IN SAGITTARIUS DAYS

DO

★ walk rather than drive to your destination

★ practise positive visualization to attract good things into your life

★ gentle stretching exercises to open up your hips and lengthen your thigh muscles

★ find time to watch an engrossing documentary

★ go horse riding

DON'T

☆ have any surgical interventions on your thighs or hips

☆ overdo any food or drink that can make you feel liverish

☆ forget the life-enhancing qualities of a good book

☆ spend too long in one place if you can avoid it

MOON IN CAPRICORN DAYS

DO

★ remind yourself that there's more to
life than work

★ gentle exercises that increase your
bone density

★ go for a walk in a beautiful wood or park

★ hug a tree

★ counteract worries with constructive
activities

DON'T

☆ have any surgical interventions on
your bones or knees

☆ lose sight of your main priorities in life

☆ neglect your appearance, even if you're busy

☆ wear your oldest or tattiest clothes, unless
you're doing something messy

MOON IN AQUARIUS DAYS

DO

★ have homeopathic treatment

★ gentle exercises to firm up your calves
or strengthen your ankles

★ write down a wish list and keep it under
your pillow

★ put a house plant by your computer to
combat its electromagnetic frequencies

DON'T

☆ underestimate the healing power of friendship

☆ have any surgical interventions on your calves
or ankles

☆ be resistant to the idea of a new beauty
treatment

☆ forget to clean your contact lenses or glasses

MOON IN PISCES DAYS

DO

★ have a reflexology or aromatherapy
treatment

★ give yourself a pedicure

★ try some qigong exercises and
breathing techniques

★ relax in a scented bath by candlelight

★ ground yourself by walking on the grass
or beach with bare feet

DON'T

☆ have any surgical interventions on your feet

☆ keep on the go if you feel tired and need a rest

☆ drain your energy by dwelling on bad news
you can't do anything about

☆ tell yourself that you're too busy to do some
mindfulness meditation

The Moon's nodes

The tables on the following pages show the dates
when the North Node (NN) and South Node (SN) of
the Moon each enter a new sign. Look up the date that
you want to check so you can see which sign the North
Node and South Node occupied at that time. If you
were born on a day when the North Node and South
Node moved signs, you can consult an astrologer or
online birth chart calculator to discover exactly which
set of signs apply to you. If you don't know your time of
birth, you can read the relevant combinations of signs
on pages 68–71 to see which ones resonate most closely
with you. You can then be fairly confident that these are
the signs of your North Node and South Node.

Example

If you were born on 20 September 1984,
look down the list and you'll see that the
North Node was in Taurus from 12
September 1984 to 6 April 1986 and the
South Node was in Scorpio. Therefore, your
North Node is in Taurus and South Node
is in Scorpio.

1 Jan 1920–6 Feb 1921	NN SCO	SN TAU
6 Feb 1921–23 Aug 1922	NN LIB	SN ARI
23 Aug 1922–28 Aug 1922	NN VIR	SN PIS
28 Aug 1922–31 Aug 1922	NN LIB	SN ARI
31 Aug 1922–23 Apr 1924	NN VIR	SN PIS
23 Apr 1924–26 Oct 1925	NN LEO	SN AQU
26 Oct 1925–16 Apr 1927	NN CAN	SN CAP
16 Apr 1927–29 Dec 1928	NN GEM	SN SAG
29 Dec 1928–8 Jul 1930	NN TAU	SN SCO
8 Jul 1930–29 Dec 1931	NN ARI	SN LIB
29 Dec 1931–25 Jun 1933	NN PIS	SN VIR
25 Jun 1933–8 Mar 1935	NN AQU	SN LEO
8 Mar 1935–15 Sep 1936	NN CAP	SN CAN
15 Sep 1936–4 Mar 1938	NN SAG	SN GEM
4 Mar 1938–12 Sep 1939	NN SCO	SN TAU
12 Sep 1939–24 May 1941	NN LIB	SN ARI
24 May 1941–21 Nov 1942	NN VIR	SN PIS
21 Nov 1942–11 May 1944	NN LEO	SN AQU
11 May 1944–3 Dec 1945	NN CAN	SN CAP
3 Dec 1945–12 Dec 1945	NN GEM	SN SAG
12 Dec 1945–14 Dec 1945	NN CAN	SN CAP
14 Dec 1945–1 Jan 1946	NN GEM	SN SAG
1 Jan 1946–4 Jan 1946	NN CAN	SN CAP
4 Jan 1946–2 Aug 1947	NN GEM	SN SAG
2 Aug 1947–26 Jan 1949	NN TAU	SN SCO
26 Jan 1949–27 Jul 1950	NN ARI	SN LIB
27 Jul 1950–28 Mar 1952	NN PIS	SN VIR

28 Mar 1952–9 Oct 1953	NN AQU	SN LEO
9 Oct 1953–3 Apr 1955	NN CAP	SN CAN
3 Apr 1955–4 Oct 1956	NN SAG	SN GEM
4 Oct 1956–16 Jun 1958	NN SCO	SN TAU
16 Jun 1958–16 Dec 1959	NN LIB	SN ARI
16 Dec 1959–11 June 1961	NN VIR	SN PIS
11 June 1961–23 Dec 1962	NN LEO	SN AQU
23 Dec 1962–26 Aug 1964	NN CAN	SN CAP
26 Aug 1964–20 Feb 1966	NN GEM	SN SAG
20 Feb 1966–20 Aug 1967	NN TAU	SN SCO
20 Aug 1967–19 Apr 1969	NN ARI	SN LIB
19 Apr 1969–2 Nov 1970	NN PIS	SN VIR
2 Nov 1970–27 Apr 1972	NN AQU	SN LEO
27 Apr 1972–27 Oct 1973	NN CAP	SN CAN
27 Oct 1973–10 Jul 1975	NN SAG	SN GEM
10 Jul 1975–8 Jan 1977	NN SCO	SN TAU
8 Jan 1977–6 Jul 1978	NN LIB	SN ARI
6 Jul 1978–13 Jan 1980	NN VIR	SN PIS
13 Jan 1980–24 Sep 1981	NN LEO	SN AQU
24 Sep 1981–16 Mar 1983	NN CAN	SN CAP
16 Mar 1983–12 Sep 1984	NN GEM	SN SAG
12 Sep 1984–6 Apr 1986	NN TAU	SN SCO
6 Apr 1986–2 Dec 1987	NN ARI	SN LIB
2 Dec 1987–23 May 1989	NN PIS	SN VIR
23 May 1989–19 Nov 1990	NN AQU	SN LEO
19 Nov 1990–2 Aug 1992	NN CAP	SN CAN

2 Aug 1992–1 Feb 1994	NN SAG	SN GEM
1 Feb 1994–1 Aug 1995	NN SCO	SN TAU
1 Aug 1995–25 Jan 1997	NN LIB	SN ARI
25 Jan 1997–20 Oct 1998	NN VIR	SN PIS
20 Oct 1998–9 Apr 2000	NN LEO	SN AQU
9 Apr 2000–13 Oct 2001	NN CAN	SN CAP
13 Oct 2001–14 Apr 2003	NN GEM	SN SAG
14 Apr 2003–26 Dec 2004	NN TAU	SN SCO
26 Dec 2004–22 Jun 2006	NN ARI	SN LIB
22 Jun 2006–18 Dec 2007	NN PIS	SN VIR
18 Dec 2007–21 Aug 2009	NN AQU	SN LEO
21 Aug 2009–3 Mar 2011	NN CAP	SN CAN
3 Mar 2011–30 Aug 2012	NN SAG	SN GEM
30 Aug 2012–18 Feb 2014	NN SCO	SN TAU
18 Feb 2014–12 Nov 2015	NN LIB	SN ARI
12 Nov 2015–9 May 2017	NN VIR	SN PIS
9 May 2017–6 Nov 2018	NN LEO	SN AQU
6 Nov 2018–5 May 2020	NN CAN	SN CAP
5 May 2020–18 Jan 2022	NN GEM	SN SAG
18 Jan 2022–17 Jul 2023	NN TAU	SN SCO
17 Jul 2023–11 Jan 2025	NN ARI	SN LIB
11 Jan 2025–26 Jul 2026	NN PIS	SN VIR
26 Jul 2026–26 Mar 2028	NN AQU	SN LEO
26 Mar 2028–23 Sep 2029	NN CAP	SN CAN
23 Sep 2029–20 Mar 2031	NN SAG	SN GEM
20 Mar 2031–1 Dec 2032	NN SCO	SN TAU

Moon tables

This section lists the eight phases of the Moon from 2019 to 2032. It provides you with an instant reference table whenever you want to check the dates of the new or full moon, or any of the other lunar phases that occur every 29 days (eclipses are shown in bold).

These tables are easy to use. The first column lists the phase of the Moon; the second column gives the date on which this phase becomes exact; the third column gives the time by GMT when this phase becomes exact; and the fourth column gives the sign in which the phase occurred, followed by the element. Eclipses are shown in bold, so they're easy to identify at a glance. The fact that these tables give times in GMT means that you'll have to convert the time of an event in any non-GMT time zone back to GMT before using the tables.

For instance, let's say that you want to know the Moon phase for the birth of your child, who was born on 21 November 2019 in the UK. First, you turn to the tables for 2019, and then search for November. There was a last quarter moon on 19 November, which became exact in Leo at 21:11 GMT. The next phase was the balsamic moon, which became exact at 06:14 in Libra on 23 November – but that's after your child was born. Therefore, your child was born towards the end of the last quarter moon phase. If you want to know the sign that the Moon occupied on that day (you'll know it's either Leo, Virgo or Libra, because you can see that these are the three signs that span the last quarter and balsamic moons in November 2019), you can refer to the Moon-sign finder tables on pages 26–9 If your child was born in a country that does not use the GMT time zone, you'll have to convert their birth time into GMT (see page 173) before consulting these tables. For instance, if your child was born in France, which is one hour ahead of GMT, you'll have to deduct one hour from their birth time to convert it to GMT.

KEY TO ABBREVIATIONS

NEW	new moon
CRES	crescent moon
FIRST	first quarter moon
GIBB	gibbous moon
FULL	full moon
DISS	disseminating moon
LAST	last quarter moon
BALS	balsamic moon
ARI	Aries
TAU	Taurus
GEM	Gemini
CAN	Cancer
LEO	Leo
VIR	Virgo
LIB	Libra
SCO	Scorpio
SAG	Sagittarius
CAP	Capricorn
AQU	Aquarius
PIS	Pisces

PHASE	DATE	GMT	SIGN/ELEMENT	PHASE	DATE	GMT	SIGN/ELEMENT
BALS	Jan 2 2019	02:07	SCO/WATER	GIBB	May 15 2019	10:30	LIB/AIR
NEW	**Jan 6 2019**	**01:29**	**CAP/EARTH**	FULL	May 18 2019	21:12	SCO/WATER
CRES	Jan 10 2019	05:12	PIS/WATER	DISS	May 22 2019	14:53	CAP/EARTH
FIRST	Jan 14 2019	06:46	ARI/FIRE	LAST	May 26 2019	16:34	PIS/WATER
GIBB	Jan 17 2019	22:35	GEM/AIR	BALS	May 30 2019	17:22	ARI/FIRE
FULL	**Jan 21 2019**	**05:17**	**LEO/FIRE**				
DISS	Jan 24 2019	10:08	VIR/EARTH	NEW	Jun 3 2019	10:02	GEM/AIR
LAST	Jan 27 2019	21:11	SCO/WATER	CRES	Jun 6 2019	20:43	LEO/FIRE
BALS	Jan 31 2019	18:00	SAG/FIRE	FIRST	Jun 10 2019	06:00	VIR/EARTH
				GIBB	Jun 13 2019	16:57	SCO/WATER
NEW	Feb 4 2019	21:04	AQU/AIR	FULL	Jun 17 2019	08:31	SAG/FIRE
CRES	Feb 9 2019	00:27	ARI/FIRE	DISS	Jun 21 2019	07:07	AQU/AIR
FIRST	Feb 12 2019	22:27	TAU/EARTH	LAST	Jun 25 2019	09:47	ARI/FIRE
GIBB	Feb 16 2019	10:53	CAN/WATER	BALS	Jun 29 2019	07:12	TAU/EARTH
FULL	Feb 19 2019	15:53	VIR/EARTH	**NEW**	**Jul 2 2019**	**19:17**	**CAN/WATER**
DISS	Feb 22 2019	21:18	LIB/AIR	CRES	Jul 6 2019	02:24	LEO/FIRE
LAST	Feb 26 2019	11:28	SAG/FIRE	FIRST	Jul 9 2019	10:55	LIB/AIR
				GIBB	Jul 13 2019	00:58	SAG/FIRE
BALS	Mar 2 2019	12:14	CAP/EARTH	**FULL**	**Jul 16 2019**	**21:39**	**CAP/EARTH**
NEW	Mar 6 2019	16:04	PIS/WATER	DISS	Jul 20 2019	23:34	PIS/WATER
CRES	Mar 10 2019	16:24	TAU/EARTH	LAST	Jul 25 2019	01:18	TAU/EARTH
FIRST	Mar 14 2019	10:28	GEM/AIR	BALS	Jul 28 2019	18:59	GEM/AIR
GIBB	Mar 17 2019	20:37	LEO/FIRE				
FULL	Mar 21 2019	01:43	LIB/AIR	NEW	Aug 1 2019	03:11	LEO/FIRE
DISS	Mar 24 2019	09:43	SCO/WATER	CRES	Aug 4 2019	08:07	VIR/EARTH
LAST	Mar 28 2019	04:10	CAP/EARTH	FIRST	Aug 7 2019	17:31	SCO/WATER
BALS	Apr 1 2019	07:15	AQU/AIR	GIBB	Aug 11 2019	11:39	CAP/EARTH
NEW	Apr 5 2019	08:51	ARI/FIRE	FULL	Aug 15 2019	12:30	AQU/AIR
CRES	Apr 9 2019	04:42	GEM/AIR	DISS	Aug 19 2019	15:28	ARI/FIRE
FIRST	Apr 12 2019	19:06	CAN/WATER	LAST	Aug 23 2019	14:57	GEM/AIR
GIBB	Apr 16 2019	04:09	VIR/EARTH	BALS	Aug 27 2019	05:06	CAN/WATER
FULL	Apr 19 2019	11:13	LIB/AIR	NEW	Aug 30 2019	10:38	VIR/EARTH
DISS	Apr 22 2019	23:35	SAG/FIRE				
LAST	Apr 26 2019	22:19	AQU/AIR	CRES	Sep 2 2019	15:06	LIB/AIR
				FIRST	Sep 6 2019	03:11	SAG/FIRE
BALS	May 1 2019	01:18	PIS/WATER	GIBB	Sep 10 2019	01:33	AQU/AIR
NEW	May 4 2019	22:46	TAU/EARTH	FULL	Sep 14 2019	04:33	PIS/WATER
CRES	May 8 2019	13:51	CAN/WATER	DISS	Sep 18 2019	06:20	TAU/EARTH
FIRST	May 12 2019	01:13	LEO/FIRE	LAST	Sep 22 2019	02:40	GEM/AIR

PHASE	DATE	GMT	SIGN/ELEMENT
BALS	Sep 25 2019	13:56	LEO/FIRE
NEW	Sep 28 2019	18:27	LIB/AIR
CRES	Oct 2 2019	00:40	SCO/WATER
FIRST	Oct 5 2019	16:48	CAP/EARTH
GIBB	Oct 9 2019	18:28	PIS/WATER
FULL	Oct 13 2019	21:08	ARI/FIRE
DISS	Oct 17 2019	19:52	GEM/AIR
LAST	Oct 21 2019	12:40	CAN/WATER
BALS	Oct 24 2019	22:02	VIR/EARTH
NEW	Oct 28 2019	03:38	SCO/WATER
CRES	Oct 31 2019	13:42	SAG/FIRE
FIRST	Nov 4 2019	10:24	AQU/AIR
GIBB	Nov 8 2019	13:30	ARI/FIRE
FULL	Nov 12 2019	13:35	TAU/EARTH
DISS	Nov 16 2019	07:55	CAN/WATER
LAST	Nov 19 2019	21:11	LEO/FIRE
BALS	Nov 23 2019	06:14	LIB/AIR
NEW	Nov 26 2019	15:05	SAG/FIRE
CRES	Nov 30 2019	06:25	CAP/EARTH
FIRST	Dec 4 2019	06:59	PIS/WATER
GIBB	Dec 8 2019	09:24	TAU/EARTH
FULL	Dec 12 2019	05:13	GEM/AIR
DISS	Dec 15 2019	18:32	LEO/FIRE
LAST	Dec 19 2019	04:58	VIR/EARTH
BALS	Dec 22 2019	15:26	SCO/WATER
NEW	**Dec 26 2019**	**05:13**	**CAP/EARTH**
CRES	Dec 30 2019	01:58	AQU/AIR
FIRST	Jan 3 2020	04:46	ARI/FIRE
GIBB	Jan 7 2020	04:40	GEM/AIR
FULL	**Jan 10 2020**	**19:22**	**CAN/WATER**
DISS	Jan 14 2020	04:00	VIR/EARTH
LAST	Jan 17 2020	12:59	LIB/AIR
BALS	Jan 21 2020	02:29	SAG/FIRE
NEW	Jan 24 2020	21:42	AQU/AIR
CRES	Jan 28 2020	22:39	PIS/WATER

PHASE	DATE	GMT	SIGN/ELEMENT
FIRST	Feb 2 2020	01:42	TAU/EARTH
GIBB	Feb 5 2020	21:49	CAN/WATER
FULL	Feb 9 2020	07:33	LEO/FIRE
DISS	Feb 12 2020	12:57	LIB/AIR
LAST	Feb 15 2020	22:18	SCO/WATER
BALS	Feb 19 2020	15:45	CAP/EARTH
NEW	Feb 23 2020	15:32	PIS/WATER
CRES	Feb 27 2020	18:38	ARI/FIRE
FIRST	Mar 2 2020	19:58	GEM/AIR
GIBB	Mar 6 2020	11:48	LEO/FIRE
FULL	Mar 9 2020	17:48	VIR/EARTH
DISS	Mar 12 2020	22:05	SCO/WATER
LAST	Mar 16 2020	09:35	SAG/FIRE
BALS	Mar 20 2020	06:58	AQU/AIR
NEW	Mar 24 2020	09:29	ARI/FIRE
CRES	Mar 28 2020	12:19	TAU/EARTH
FIRST	Apr 1 2020	10:22	CAN/WATER
GIBB	Apr 4 2020	22:18	VIR/EARTH
FULL	Apr 8 2020	02:36	LIB/AIR
DISS	Apr 11 2020	08:06	SAG/FIRE
LAST	Apr 14 2020	22:57	CAP/EARTH
BALS	Apr 18 2020	23:24	PIS/WATER
NEW	Apr 23 2020	02:26	TAU/EARTH
CRES	Apr 27 2020	02:46	GEM/AIR
FIRST	Apr 30 2020	20:39	LEO/FIRE
GIBB	May 4 2020	05:56	VIR/EARTH
FULL	May 7 2020	10:45	SCO/WATER
DISS	May 10 2020	19:24	CAP/EARTH
LAST	May 14 2020	14:03	AQU/AIR
BALS	May 18 2020	16:16	ARI/FIRE
NEW	May 22 2020	17:39	GEM/AIR
CRES	May 26 2020	13:45	CAN/WATER
FIRST	May 30 2020	03:30	VIR/EARTH
GIBB	Jun 2 2020	11:50	LIB/AIR
FULL	**Jun 5 2020**	**19:13**	**SAG/FIRE**

PHASE	DATE	GMT	SIGN/ELEMENT
DISS	Jun 9 2020	08:10	AQU/AIR
LAST	Jun 13 2020	06:24	PIS/WATER
BALS	Jun 17 2020	08:51	TAU/EARTH
NEW	**Jun 21 2020**	**06:42**	**CAN/WATER**
CRES	Jun 24 2020	21:42	LEO/FIRE
FIRST	Jun 28 2020	08:16	LIB/AIR
GIBB	Jul 1 2020	17:26	SCO/WATER
FULL	**Jul 5 2020**	**04:44**	**CAP/EARTH**
DISS	Jul 8 2020	22:26	PIS/WATER
LAST	Jul 12 2020	23:29	ARI/FIRE
BALS	Jul 17 2020	00:32	GEM/AIR
NEW	Jul 20 2020	17:33	CAN/WATER
CRES	Jul 24 2020	03:42	VIR/EARTH
FIRST	Jul 27 2020	12:33	SCO/WATER
GIBB	Jul 31 2020	00:02	SAG/FIRE
FULL	Aug 3 2020	15:59	AQU/AIR
DISS	Aug 7 2020	14:07	ARI/FIRE
LAST	Aug 11 2020	16:45	TAU/EARTH
BALS	Aug 15 2020	14:48	CAN/WATER
NEW	Aug 19 2020	02:41	LEO/FIRE
CRES	Aug 22 2020	09:14	LIB/AIR
FIRST	Aug 25 2020	17:58	SAG/FIRE
GIBB	Aug 29 2020	08:47	CAP/EARTH
FULL	Sep 2 2020	05:22	PIS/WATER
DISS	Sep 6 2020	07:00	ARI/FIRE
LAST	Sep 10 2020	09:26	GEM/AIR
BALS	Sep 14 2020	03:24	LEO/FIRE
NEW	Sep 17 2020	11:00	VIR/EARTH
CRES	Sep 20 2020	15:44	SCO/WATER
FIRST	Sep 24 2020	01:55	CAP/EARTH
GIBB	Sep 27 2020	20:33	AQU/AIR
FULL	Oct 1 2020	21:06	ARI/FIRE
DISS	Oct 6 2020	00:26	TAU/EARTH
LAST	Oct 10 2020	00:40	CAN/WATER
BALS	Oct 13 2020	14:29	VIR/EARTH

PHASE	DATE	GMT	SIGN/ELEMENT
NEW	Oct 16 2020	19:31	LIB/AIR
CRES	Oct 20 2020	00:29	SAG/FIRE
FIRST	Oct 23 2020	13:23	AQU/AIR
GIBB	Oct 27 2020	11:48	PIS/WATER
FULL	Oct 31 2020	14:50	TAU/EARTH
DISS	Nov 4 2020	17:20	GEM/AIR
LAST	Nov 8 2020	13:47	LEO/FIRE
BALS	Nov 12 2020	00:26	LIB/AIR
NEW	Nov 15 2020	05:07	SCO/WATER
CRES	Nov 18 2020	12:13	CAP/EARTH
FIRST	Nov 22 2020	04:45	PIS/WATER
GIBB	Nov 26 2020	06:20	ARI/FIRE
FULL	**Nov 30 2020**	**09:30**	**GEM/AIR**
DISS	Dec 4 2020	08:28	CAN/WATER
LAST	Dec 8 2020	00:36	VIR/EARTH
BALS	Dec 11 2020	09:51	SCO/WATER
NEW	**Dec 14 2020**	**16:17**	**SAG/FIRE**
CRES	Dec 18 2020	03:02	AQU/AIR
FIRST	Dec 21 2020	23:42	ARI/FIRE
GIBB	Dec 26 2020	03:03	TAU/EARTH
FULL	Dec 30 2020	03:29	CAN/WATER
DISS	Jan 2 2021	21:07	LEO/FIRE
LAST	Jan 6 2021	09:37	LIB/AIR
BALS	Jan 9 2021	19:12	SAG/FIRE
NEW	Jan 13 2021	05:01	CAP/EARTH
CRES	Jan 16 2021	20:30	PIS/WATER
FIRST	Jan 20 2021	21:02	TAU/EARTH
GIBB	Jan 24 2021	23:54	GEM/AIR
FULL	Jan 28 2021	19:16	LEO/FIRE
DISS	Feb 1 2021	07:26	VIR/EARTH
LAST	Feb 4 2021	17:37	SCO/WATER
BALS	Feb 8 2021	04:55	CAP/EARTH
NEW	Feb 11 2021	19:06	AQU/AIR
CRES	Feb 15 2021	15:40	ARI/FIRE
FIRST	Feb 19 2021	18:48	GEM/AIR

PHASE	DATE	GMT	SIGN/ELEMENT
GIBB	Feb 23 2021	18:41	CAN/WATER
FULL	Feb 27 2021	08:18	VIR/EARTH
DISS	Mar 2 2021	16:11	LIB/AIR
LAST	Mar 6 2021	01:30	SAG/FIRE
BALS	Mar 9 2021	15:26	AQU/AIR
NEW	Mar 13 2021	10:22	PIS/WATER
CRES	Mar 17 2021	11:21	TAU/EARTH
FIRST	Mar 21 2021	14:41	CAN/WATER
GIBB	Mar 25 2021	10:00	LEO/FIRE
FULL	Mar 28 2021	18:48	LIB/AIR
DISS	Apr 1 2021	00:14	SCO/WATER
LAST	Apr 4 2021	10:02	CAP/EARTH
BALS	Apr 8 2021	03:09	PIS/WATER
NEW	Apr 12 2021	02:31	ARI/FIRE
CRES	Apr 16 2021	05:58	GEM/AIR
FIRST	Apr 20 2021	06:59	LEO/FIRE
GIBB	Apr 23 2021	21:44	VIR/EARTH
FULL	Apr 27 2021	03:31	SCO/WATER
DISS	Apr 30 2021	08:23	SAG/FIRE
LAST	May 3 2021	19:50	AQU/AIR
BALS	May 7 2021	16:28	ARI/FIRE
NEW	May 11 2021	19:00	TAU/EARTH
CRES	May 15 2021	22:04	CAN/WATER
FIRST	May 19 2021	19:13	LEO/FIRE
GIBB	May 23 2021	06:30	LIB/AIR
FULL	**May 26 2021**	**11:14**	**SAG/FIRE**
DISS	May 29 2021	17:08	CAP/EARTH
LAST	Jun 2 2021	07:25	PIS/WATER
BALS	Jun 6 2021	07:26	TAU/EARTH
NEW	**Jun 10 2021**	**10:53**	**GEM/AIR**
CRES	Jun 14 2021	10:54	LEO/FIRE
FIRST	Jun 18 2021	03:55	VIR/EARTH
GIBB	Jun 21 2021	13:16	SCO/WATER
FULL	Jun 24 2021	18:39	CAP/EARTH
DISS	Jun 28 2021	03:07	AQU/AIR

PHASE	DATE	GMT	SIGN/ELEMENT
LAST	Jul 1 2021	21:11	ARI/FIRE
BALS	Jul 5 2021	23:40	TAU/EARTH
NEW	Jul 10 2021	01:17	CAN/WATER
CRES	Jul 13 2021	20:41	VIR/EARTH
FIRST	Jul 17 2021	10:11	LIB/AIR
GIBB	Jul 20 2021	19:06	SAG/FIRE
FULL	Jul 24 2021	02:37	AQU/AIR
DISS	Jul 27 2021	15:01	PIS/WATER
LAST	Jul 31 2021	13:16	TAU/EARTH
BALS	Aug 4 2021	16:19	GEM/AIR
NEW	Aug 8 2021	13:51	LEO/FIRE
CRES	Aug 12 2021	04:19	LIB/AIR
FIRST	Aug 15 2021	15:20	SCO/WATER
GIBB	Aug 19 2021	01:03	CAP/EARTH
FULL	Aug 22 2021	12:02	AQU/AIR
DISS	Aug 26 2021	05:27	ARI/FIRE
LAST	Aug 30 2021	07:14	GEM/AIR
BALS	Sep 3 2021	08:29	CAN/WATER
NEW	Sep 7 2021	00:52	VIR/EARTH
CRES	Sep 10 2021	11:04	SCO/WATER
FIRST	Sep 13 2021	20:40	SAG/FIRE
GIBB	Sep 17 2021	08:19	AQU/AIR
FULL	Sep 20 2021	23:55	PIS/WATER
DISS	Sep 24 2021	22:33	TAU/EARTH
LAST	Sep 29 2021	01:58	CAN/WATER
BALS	Oct 2 2021	23:35	LEO/FIRE
NEW	Oct 6 2021	11:06	LIB/AIR
CRES	Oct 9 2021	18:08	SAG/FIRE
FIRST	Oct 13 2021	03:26	CAP/EARTH
GIBB	Oct 16 2021	18:06	PIS/WATER
FULL	Oct 20 2021	14:57	ARI/FIRE
DISS	Oct 24 2021	17:33	GEM/AIR
LAST	Oct 28 2021	20:06	LEO/FIRE
BALS	Nov 1 2021	13:29	VIR/EARTH

PHASE	DATE	GMT	SIGN/ELEMENT
NEW	Nov 4 2021	21:15	SCO/WATER
CRES	Nov 8 2021	02:32	CAP/EARTH
FIRST	Nov 11 2021	12:46	AQU/AIR
GIBB	Nov 15 2021	07:28	ARI/FIRE
FULL	**Nov 19 2021**	**08:58**	**TAU/EARTH**
DISS	Nov 23 2021	12:51	CAN/WATER
LAST	Nov 27 2021	12:28	VIR/EARTH
BALS	Dec 1 2021	02:08	LIB/AIR
NEW	**Dec 4 2021**	**07:43**	**SAG/FIRE**
CRES	Dec 7 2021	12:51	AQU/AIR
FIRST	Dec 11 2021	01:36	PIS/WATER
GIBB	Dec 15 2021	00:41	TAU/EARTH
FULL	Dec 19 2021	04:36	GEM/AIR
DISS	Dec 23 2021	06:37	LEO/FIRE
LAST	Dec 27 2021	02:24	LIB/AIR
BALS	Dec 30 2021	13:29	SCO/WATER
NEW	Jan 2 2022	18:33	CAP/EARTH
CRES	Jan 6 2022	01:27	PIS/WATER
FIRST	Jan 9 2022	18:12	ARI/FIRE
GIBB	Jan 13 2022	20:45	GEM/AIR
FULL	Jan 17 2022	23:49	CAN/WATER
DISS	Jan 21 2022	21:42	VIR/EARTH
LAST	Jan 25 2022	13:40	SCO/WATER
BALS	Jan 28 2022	23:23	SAG/FIRE
NEW	Feb 1 2022	05:45	AQU/AIR
CRES	Feb 4 2022	16:26	ARI/FIRE
FIRST	Feb 8 2022	13:50	TAU/EARTH
GIBB	Feb 12 2022	17:34	CAN/WATER
FULL	Feb 16 2022	16:57	LEO/FIRE
DISS	Feb 20 2022	09:50	LIB/AIR
LAST	Feb 23 2022	22:32	SAG/FIRE
BALS	Feb 27 2022	08:06	CAP/EARTH
NEW	Mar 2 2022	17:35	PIS/WATER
CRES	Mar 6 2022	09:30	TAU/EARTH
FIRST	Mar 10 2022	10:46	GEM/AIR
GIBB	Mar 14 2022	12:57	LEO/FIRE
FULL	Mar 18 2022	07:18	VIR/EARTH
DISS	Mar 21 2022	19:25	SCO/WATER
LAST	Mar 25 2022	05:38	CAP/EARTH
BALS	Mar 28 2022	16:20	AQU/AIR
NEW	Apr 1 2022	06:25	ARI/FIRE
CRES	Apr 5 2022	03:46	GEM/AIR
FIRST	Apr 9 2022	06:48	CAN/WATER
GIBB	Apr 13 2022	05:34	VIR/EARTH
FULL	Apr 16 2022	18:55	LIB/AIR
DISS	Apr 20 2022	03:05	SAG/FIRE
LAST	Apr 23 2022	11:56	AQU/AIR
BALS	Apr 27 2022	01:10	PIS/WATER
NEW	**Apr 30 2022**	**20:28**	**TAU/EARTH**
CRES	May 4 2022	21:54	GEM/AIR
FIRST	May 9 2022	00:22	LEO/FIRE
GIBB	May 12 2022	19:05	LIB/AIR
FULL	**May 16 2022**	**04:15**	**SCO/WATER**
DISS	May 19 2022	09:42	CAP/EARTH
LAST	May 22 2022	18:43	PIS/WATER
BALS	May 26 2022	11:36	ARI/FIRE
NEW	May 30 2022	11:31	GEM/AIR
CRES	Jun 3 2022	14:37	CAN/WATER
FIRST	Jun 7 2022	14:49	VIR/EARTH
GIBB	Jun 11 2022	05:44	SCO/WATER
FULL	Jun 14 2022	11:51	SAG/FIRE
DISS	Jun 17 2022	16:16	AQU/AIR
LAST	Jun 21 2022	03:10	PIS/WATER
BALS	Jun 25 2022	00:10	TAU/EARTH
NEW	Jun 29 2022	02:53	CAN/WATER
CRES	Jul 3 2022	05:12	LEO/FIRE
FIRST	Jul 7 2022	02:15	LIB/AIR
GIBB	Jul 10 2022	14:03	SAG/FIRE
FULL	Jul 13 2022	18:38	CAP/EARTH
DISS	Jul 16 2022	23:56	PIS/WATER

PHASE	DATE	GMT	SIGN/ELEMENT
LAST	Jul 20 2022	14:19	ARI/FIRE
BALS	Jul 24 2022	14:53	GEM/AIR
NEW	Jul 28 2022	17:55	LEO/FIRE
CRES	Aug 1 2022	17:33	VIR/EARTH
FIRST	Aug 5 2022	11:07	SCO/WATER
GIBB	Aug 8 2022	20:45	CAP/EARTH
FULL	Aug 12 2022	01:36	AQU/AIR
DISS	Aug 15 2022	09:52	ARI/FIRE
LAST	Aug 19 2022	04:36	TAU/EARTH
BALS	Aug 23 2022	07:15	CAN/WATER
NEW	Aug 27 2022	08:17	VIR/EARTH
CRES	Aug 31 2022	03:58	LIB/AIR
FIRST	Sep 3 2022	18:08	SAG/FIRE
GIBB	Sep 7 2022	02:51	CAP/EARTH
FULL	Sep 10 2022	09:59	PIS/WATER
DISS	Sep 13 2022	22:55	TAU/EARTH
LAST	Sep 17 2022	21:52	GEM/AIR
BALS	Sep 22 2022	00:34	LEO/FIRE
NEW	Sep 25 2022	21:55	LIB/AIR
CRES	Sep 29 2022	13:00	SCO/WATER
FIRST	Oct 3 2022	00:14	CAP/EARTH
GIBB	Oct 6 2022	09:37	AQU/AIR
FULL	Oct 9 2022	20:55	ARI/FIRE
DISS	Oct 13 2022	15:19	GEM/AIR
LAST	Oct 17 2022	17:15	CAN/WATER
BALS	Oct 21 2022	18:07	VIR/EARTH
NEW	**Oct 25 2022**	**10:49**	**SCO/WATER**
CRES	Oct 28 2022	21:20	SAG/FIRE
FIRST	Nov 1 2022	06:36	AQU/AIR
GIBB	Nov 4 2022	18:22	PIS/WATER
FULL	**Nov 8 2022**	**11:03**	**TAU/EARTH**
DISS	Nov 12 2022	10:23	CAN/WATER
LAST	Nov 16 2022	13:27	LEO/FIRE
BALS	Nov 20 2022	11:08	LIB/AIR
NEW	Nov 23 2022	22:58	SAG/FIRE

PHASE	DATE	GMT	SIGN/ELEMENT
CRES	Nov 27 2022	05:41	CAP/EARTH
FIRST	Nov 30 2022	14:37	PIS/WATER
GIBB	Dec 4 2022	06:08	ARI/FIRE
FULL	Dec 8 2022	04:09	GEM/AIR
DISS	Dec 12 2022	06:41	LEO/FIRE
LAST	Dec 16 2022	08:56	VIR/EARTH
BALS	Dec 20 2022	02:40	SCO/WATER
NEW	Dec 23 2022	10:17	CAP/EARTH
CRES	Dec 26 2022	14:55	AQU/AIR
FIRST	Dec 30 2022	01:21	ARI/FIRE
GIBB	Jan 2 2023	21:17	TAU/EARTH
FULL	Jan 6 2023	23:08	CAN/WATER
DISS	Jan 11 2023	02:28	VIR/EARTH
LAST	Jan 15 2023	02:11	LIB/AIR
BALS	Jan 18 2023	15:56	SAG/FIRE
NEW	Jan 21 2023	20:54	AQU/AIR
CRES	Jan 25 2023	01:42	PIS/WATER
FIRST	Jan 28 2023	15:19	TAU/EARTH
GIBB	Feb 1 2023	15:08	GEM/AIR
FULL	Feb 5 2023	18:29	LEO/FIRE
DISS	Feb 9 2023	20:08	LIB/AIR
LAST	Feb 13 2023	16:01	SCO/WATER
BALS	Feb 17 2023	02:34	CAP/EARTH
NEW	Feb 20 2023	07:05	PIS/WATER
CRES	Feb 23 2023	14:28	ARI/FIRE
FIRST	Feb 27 2023	08:06	GEM/AIR
GIBB	Mar 3 2023	10:20	CAN/WATER
FULL	Mar 7 2023	12:41	VIR/EARTH
DISS	Mar 11 2023	10:33	SCO/WATER
LAST	Mar 15 2023	02:09	SAG/FIRE
BALS	Mar 18 2023	10:58	AQU/AIR
NEW	Mar 21 2023	17:23	ARI/FIRE
CRES	Mar 25 2023	04:59	TAU/EARTH
FIRST	Mar 29 2023	02:33	CAN/WATER

PHASE	DATE	GMT	SIGN/ELEMENT
GIBB	Apr 2 2023	05:24	LEO/FIRE
FULL	Apr 6 2023	04:34	LIB/AIR
DISS	Apr 9 2023	21:25	SAG/FIRE
LAST	Apr 13 2023	09:11	CAP/EARTH
BALS	Apr 16 2023	18:08	PIS/WATER
NEW	**Apr 20 2023**	**04:13**	**ARI/FIRE**
CRES	Apr 23 2023	20:43	GEM/AIR
FIRST	Apr 27 2023	21:20	LEO/FIRE
GIBB	May 1 2023	23:01	VIR/EARTH
FULL	**May 5 2023**	**17:34**	**SCO/WATER**
DISS	May 9 2023	05:12	CAP/EARTH
LAST	May 12 2023	14:29	AQU/AIR
BALS	May 16 2023	01:11	ARI/FIRE
NEW	May 19 2023	15:54	TAU/EARTH
CRES	May 23 2023	13:01	CAN/WATER
FIRST	May 27 2023	15:23	VIR/EARTH
GIBB	May 31 2023	14:19	LIB/AIR
FULL	Jun 4 2023	03:41	SAG/FIRE
DISS	Jun 7 2023	11:06	AQU/AIR
LAST	Jun 10 2023	19:31	PIS/WATER
BALS	Jun 14 2023	09:13	TAU/EARTH
NEW	Jun 18 2023	04:37	GEM/AIR
CRES	Jun 22 2023	05:23	LEO/FIRE
FIRST	Jun 26 2023	07:50	LIB/AIR
GIBB	Jun 30 2023	02:56	SCO/WATER
FULL	Jul 3 2023	11:39	CAP/EARTH
DISS	Jul 6 2023	16:31	AQU/AIR
LAST	Jul 10 2023	01:48	ARI/FIRE
BALS	Jul 13 2023	19:06	GEM/AIR
NEW	Jul 17 2023	18:32	CAN/WATER
CRES	Jul 21 2023	21:21	VIR/EARTH
FIRST	Jul 25 2023	22:07	SCO/WATER
GIBB	Jul 29 2023	13:02	SAG/FIRE
FULL	Aug 1 2023	18:32	AQU/AIR
DISS	Aug 4 2023	22:54	PIS/WATER

PHASE	DATE	GMT	SIGN/ELEMENT
LAST	Aug 8 2023	10:29	TAU/EARTH
BALS	Aug 12 2023	07:28	CAN/WATER
NEW	Aug 16 2023	09:39	LEO/FIRE
CRES	Aug 20 2023	12:24	LIB/AIR
FIRST	Aug 24 2023	09:58	SAG/FIRE
GIBB	Aug 27 2023	21:19	CAP/EARTH
FULL	Aug 31 2023	01:35	PIS/WATER
DISS	Sep 3 2023	07:27	ARI/FIRE
LAST	Sep 6 2023	22:21	GEM/AIR
BALS	Sep 10 2023	22:34	LEO/FIRE
NEW	Sep 15 2023	01:40	VIR/EARTH
CRES	Sep 19 2023	02:01	SCO/WATER
FIRST	Sep 22 2023	19:32	SAG/FIRE
GIBB	Sep 26 2023	04:44	AQU/FIRE
FULL	Sep 29 2023	09:58	ARI/FIRE
DISS	Oct 2 2023	19:00	TAU/EARTH
LAST	Oct 6 2023	13:48	CAN/WATER
BALS	Oct 10 2023	16:17	VIR/EARTH
NEW	**Oct 14 2023**	**17:55**	**LIB/AIR**
CRES	Oct 18 2023	13:49	SAG/FIRE
FIRST	Oct 22 2023	03:30	CAP/EARTH
GIBB	Oct 25 2023	12:21	PIS/WATER
FULL	**Oct 28 2023**	**20:24**	**TAU/EARTH**
DISS	Nov 1 2023	09:49	GEM/AIR
LAST	Nov 5 2023	08:37	LEO/FIRE
BALS	Nov 9 2023	11:44	LIB/AIR
NEW	Nov 13 2023	09:28	SCO/WATER
CRES	Nov 16 2023	23:58	CAP/EARTH
FIRST	Nov 20 2023	10:50	AQU/AIR
GIBB	Nov 23 2023	21:02	ARI/FIRE
FULL	Nov 27 2023	09:17	GEM/AIR
DISS	Dec 1 2023	03:42	CAN/WATER
LAST	Dec 5 2023	05:50	VIR/EARTH
BALS	Dec 9 2023	07:17	SCO/WATER
NEW	Dec 12 2023	23:32	SAG/FIRE

PHASE	DATE	GMT	SIGN/ELEMENT
CRES	Dec 16 2023	09:08	AQU/AIR
FIRST	Dec 19 2023	18:40	PIS/WATER
GIBB	Dec 23 2023	07:29	TAU/EARTH
FULL	Dec 27 2023	00:34	CAN/WATER
DISS	Dec 30 2023	23:51	LEO/FIRE
LAST	Jan 4 2024	03:31	LIB/AIR
BALS	Jan 8 2024	01:10	SAG/FIRE
NEW	Jan 11 2024	11:58	CAP/EARTH
CRES	Jan 14 2024	18:13	PIS/WATER
FIRST	Jan 18 2024	03:53	ARI/FIRE
GIBB	Jan 21 2024	20:02	GEM/AIR
FULL	Jan 25 2024	17:54	LEO/FIRE
DISS	Jan 29 2024	20:44	VIR/EARTH
LAST	Feb 2 2024	23:18	SCO/WATER
BALS	Feb 6 2024	16:11	CAP/EARTH
NEW	Feb 9 2024	23:00	AQU/AIR
CRES	Feb 13 2024	03:56	ARI/FIRE
FIRST	Feb 16 2024	15:01	TAU/EARTH
GIBB	Feb 20 2024	10:47	CAN/WATER
FULL	Feb 24 2024	12:31	VIR/EARTH
DISS	Feb 28 2024	16:15	LIB/AIR
LAST	Mar 3 2024	15:24	SAG/FIRE
BALS	Mar 7 2024	04:04	AQU/AIR
NEW	Mar 10 2024	09:00	PIS/WATER
CRES	Mar 13 2024	14:32	TAU/EARTH
FIRST	Mar 17 2024	04:11	GEM/AIR
GIBB	Mar 21 2024	03:28	LEO/FIRE
FULL	**Mar 25 2024**	**07:01**	**LIB/AIR**
DISS	Mar 29 2024	08:33	SCO/WATER
LAST	Apr 2 2024	03:15	CAP/EARTH
BALS	Apr 5 2024	13:14	PIS/WATER
NEW	**Apr 8 2024**	**18:20**	**ARI/FIRE**
CRES	Apr 12 2024	02:07	GEM/AIR
FIRST	Apr 15 2024	19:13	CAN/WATER
GIBB	Apr 19 2024	21:15	VIR/EARTH

PHASE	DATE	GMT	SIGN/ELEMENT
FULL	Apr 23 2024	23:49	SCO/WATER
DISS	Apr 27 2024	20:54	SAG/FIRE
LAST	May 1 2024	11:28	AQU/AIR
BALS	May 4 2024	20:26	PIS/WATER
NEW	May 8 2024	03:22	TAU/EARTH
CRES	May 11 2024	14:42	CAN/WATER
FIRST	May 15 2024	11:48	LEO/FIRE
GIBB	May 19 2024	14:55	LIB/AIR
FULL	May 23 2024	13:53	SAG/FIRE
DISS	May 27 2024	05:44	CAP/EARTH
LAST	May 30 2024	17:12	PIS/WATER
BALS	Jun 3 2024	02:36	ARI/FIRE
NEW	Jun 6 2024	12:38	GEM/AIR
CRES	Jun 10 2024	04:34	LEO/FIRE
FIRST	Jun 14 2024	05:19	VIR/EARTH
GIBB	Jun 18 2024	07:15	SCO/WATER
FULL	Jun 22 2024	01:08	CAP/EARTH
DISS	Jun 25 2024	12:15	AQU/AIR
LAST	Jun 28 2024	21:54	ARI/FIRE
BALS	Jul 2 2024	08:49	TAU/EARTH
NEW	Jul 5 2024	22:58	CAN/WATER
CRES	Jul 9 2024	19:54	VIR/EARTH
FIRST	Jul 13 2024	22:49	LIB/AIR
GIBB	Jul 17 2024	21:33	SAG/FIRE
FULL	Jul 21 2024	10:17	CAP/EARTH
DISS	Jul 24 2024	17:53	PIS/WATER
LAST	Jul 28 2024	02:52	TAU/EARTH
BALS	Jul 31 2024	16:18	GEM/AIR
NEW	Aug 4 2024	11:13	LEO/FIRE
CRES	Aug 8 2024	12:29	LIB/AIR
FIRST	Aug 12 2024	15:19	SCO/WATER
GIBB	Aug 16 2024	09:51	CAP/EARTH
FULL	Aug 19 2024	18:25	AQU/AIR
DISS	Aug 22 2024	23:54	ARI/FIRE
LAST	Aug 26 2024	09:26	GEM/AIR

PHASE	DATE	GMT	SIGN/ELEMENT	PHASE	DATE	GMT	SIGN/ELEMENT
BALS	Aug 30 2024	02:18	CAN/WATER	CRES	Jan 3 2025	12:33	AQU/AIR
				FIRST	Jan 6 2025	23:57	ARI/FIRE
NEW	Sep 3 2024	01:56	VIR/EARTH	GIBB	Jan 10 2025	10:20	GEM/AIR
CRES	Sep 7 2024	05:30	SCO/WATER	FULL	Jan 13 2025	22:27	CAN/WATER
FIRST	Sep 11 2024	06:05	SAG/FIRE	DISS	Jan 17 2025	17:36	VIR/EARTH
GIBB	Sep 14 2024	20:38	AQU/AIR	LAST	Jan 21 2025	20:31	SCO/WATER
FULL	**Sep 18 2024**	**02:35**	**PIS/WATER**	BALS	Jan 25 2025	21:13	SAG/FIRE
DISS	Sep 21 2024	07:27	TAU/EARTH	NEW	Jan 29 2025	12:36	AQU/AIR
LAST	Sep 24 2024	18:50	CAN/WATER				
BALS	Sep 28 2024	15:48	LEO/FIRE	CRES	Feb 1 2025	22:21	PIS/WATER
				FIRST	Feb 5 2025	08:01	TAU/EARTH
NEW	**Oct 2 2024**	**18:50**	**LIB/AIR**	GIBB	Feb 8 2025	20:32	CAN/WATER
CRES	Oct 6 2024	21:51	SCO/WATER	FULL	Feb 12 2025	13:54	LEO/FIRE
FIRST	Oct 10 2024	18:55	CAP/EARTH	DISS	Feb 16 2025	14:09	LIB/AIR
GIBB	Oct 14 2024	06:30	PIS/WATER	LAST	Feb 20 2025	17:33	SAG/FIRE
FULL	Oct 17 2024	11:27	ARI/FIRE	BALS	Feb 24 2025	14:06	CAP/EARTH
DISS	Oct 20 2024	17:22	GEM/AIR	NEW	Feb 28 2025	00:45	PIS/WATER
LAST	Oct 24 2024	08:03	LEO/FIRE				
BALS	Oct 28 2024	09:01	VIR/EARTH	CRES	Mar 3 2025	07:16	ARI/FIRE
				FIRST	Mar 6 2025	16:32	GEM/AIR
NEW	Nov 1 2024	12:47	SCO/WATER	GIBB	Mar 10 2025	08:20	LEO/FIRE
CRES	Nov 5 2024	12:37	SAG/FIRE	**FULL**	**Mar 14 2025**	**06:55**	**VIR/EARTH**
FIRST	Nov 9 2024	05:56	AQU/AIR	DISS	Mar 18 2025	10:01	SCO/WATER
GIBB	Nov 12 2024	15:51	ARI/FIRE	LAST	Mar 22 2025	11:30	CAP/EARTH
FULL	Nov 15 2024	21:28	TAU/EARTH	BALS	Mar 26 2025	03:49	AQU/AIR
DISS	Nov 19 2024	06:17	CAN/WATER	**NEW**	**Mar 29 2025**	**10:58**	**ARI/FIRE**
LAST	Nov 23 2024	01:28	VIR/EARTH				
BALS	Nov 27 2024	04:59	LIB/AIR	CRES	Apr 1 2025	15:47	TAU/EARTH
				FIRST	Apr 5 2025	02:14	CAN/WATER
NEW	Dec 1 2024	06:22	SAG/FIRE	GIBB	Apr 8 2025	22:07	VIR/EARTH
CRES	Dec 5 2024	01:27	CAP/EARTH	FULL	Apr 13 2025	00:23	LIB/AIR
FIRST	Dec 8 2024	15:27	PIS/WATER	DISS	Apr 17 2025	03:24	SAG/FIRE
GIBB	Dec 12 2024	00:59	TAU/EARTH	LAST	Apr 21 2025	01:36	AQU/AIR
FULL	Dec 15 2024	09:01	GEM/AIR	BALS	Apr 24 2025	14:24	PIS/WATER
DISS	Dec 18 2024	22:30	LEO/FIRE	NEW	Apr 27 2025	19:30	TAU/EARTH
LAST	Dec 22 2024	22:18	LIB/AIR				
BALS	Dec 27 2024	01:44	SCO/WATER	CRES	May 1 2025	00:32	GEM/AIR
NEW	Dec 30 2024	22:27	CAP/EARTH	FIRST	May 4 2025	13:52	LEO/FIRE
				GIBB	May 8 2025	13:36	LIB/AIR

PHASE	DATE	GMT	SIGN/ELEMENT
FULL	May 12 2025	16:56	SCO/WATER
DISS	May 16 2025	17:29	CAP/EARTH
LAST	May 20 2025	11:59	AQU/AIR
BALS	May 23 2025	22:15	ARI/FIRE
NEW	May 27 2025	03:03	GEM/AIR
CRES	May 30 2025	10:18	CAN/WATER
FIRST	Jun 3 2025	03:41	VIR/EARTH
GIBB	Jun 7 2025	05:57	SCO/WATER
FULL	Jun 11 2025	07:44	SAG/FIRE
DISS	Jun 15 2025	04:23	AQU/AIR
LAST	Jun 18 2025	19:19	PIS/WATER
BALS	Jun 22 2025	04:13	TAU/EARTH
NEW	Jun 25 2025	10:31	CAN/WATER
CRES	Jun 28 2025	21:51	LEO/FIRE
FIRST	Jul 2 2025	19:30	LIB/AIR
GIBB	Jul 6 2025	22:17	SAG/FIRE
FULL	Jul 10 2025	20:36	CAP/EARTH
DISS	Jul 14 2025	12:48	PIS/WATER
LAST	Jul 18 2025	00:38	ARI/FIRE
BALS	Jul 21 2025	09:30	GEM/AIR
NEW	Jul 24 2025	19:11	LEO/FIRE
CRES	Jul 28 2025	11:41	VIR/EARTH
FIRST	Aug 1 2025	12:42	SCO/WATER
GIBB	Aug 5 2025	14:01	SAG/FIRE
FULL	Aug 9 2025	07:55	AQU/AIR
DISS	Aug 12 2025	19:39	ARI/FIRE
LAST	Aug 16 2025	05:12	TAU/EARTH
BALS	Aug 19 2025	15:37	CAN/WATER
NEW	Aug 23 2025	06:07	VIR/EARTH
CRES	Aug 27 2025	03:45	LIB/AIR
FIRST	Aug 31 2025	06:25	SAG/FIRE
GIBB	Sep 4 2025	04:53	CAP/EARTH
FULL	**Sep 7 2025**	**18:09**	**PIS/WATER**
DISS	Sep 11 2025	01:59	TAU/EARTH
LAST	Sep 14 2025	10:33	GEM/AIR
BALS	Sep 18 2025	00:04	LEO/FIRE
NEW	**Sep 21 2025**	**19:54**	**VIR/EARTH**
CRES	Sep 25 2025	21:26	SCO/WATER
FIRST	Sep 29 2025	23:54	CAP/EARTH
GIBB	Oct 3 2025	18:47	AQU/AIR
FULL	Oct 7 2025	03:48	ARI/FIRE
DISS	Oct 10 2025	08:57	GEM/AIR
LAST	Oct 13 2025	18:12	CAN/WATER
BALS	Oct 17 2025	11:57	VIR/EARTH
NEW	Oct 21 2025	12:25	LIB/AIR
CRES	Oct 25 2025	15:43	SAG/FIRE
FIRST	Oct 29 2025	16:21	AQU/AIR
GIBB	Nov 2 2025	07:30	PIS/WATER
FULL	Nov 5 2025	13:20	TAU/EARTH
DISS	Nov 8 2025	17:40	CAN/WATER
LAST	Nov 12 2025	05:28	LEO/FIRE
BALS	Nov 16 2025	03:39	LIB/AIR
NEW	Nov 20 2025	06:48	SCO/WATER
CRES	Nov 24 2025	09:25	CAP/EARTH
FIRST	Nov 28 2025	06:59	PIS/WATER
GIBB	Dec 1 2025	18:49	ARI/FIRE
FULL	Dec 4 2025	23:13	GEM/AIR
DISS	Dec 8 2025	05:05	LEO/FIRE
LAST	Dec 11 2025	20:52	VIR/EARTH
BALS	Dec 15 2025	22:30	SCO/WATER
NEW	Dec 20 2025	01:44	SAG/FIRE
CRES	Dec 24 2025	01:30	AQU/AIR
FIRST	Dec 27 2025	19:10	ARI/FIRE
GIBB	Dec 31 2025	04:44	TAU/EARTH
FULL	Jan 3 2026	10:02	CAN/WATER
DISS	Jan 6 2026	19:36	VIR/EARTH
LAST	Jan 10 2026	15:49	LIB/AIR
BALS	Jan 14 2026	19:01	SAG/FIRE
NEW	Jan 18 2026	19:52	CAP/EARTH
CRES	Jan 22 2026	15:06	PIS/WATER

PHASE	DATE	GMT	SIGN/ELEMENT
FIRST	Jan 26 2026	04:48	TAU/EARTH
GIBB	Jan 29 2026	13:44	GEM/AIR
FULL	Feb 1 2026	22:10	LEO/FIRE
DISS	Feb 5 2026	12:46	LIB/AIR
LAST	Feb 9 2026	12:43	SCO/WATER
BALS	Feb 13 2026	15:23	CAP/EARTH
NEW	**Feb 17 2026**	**12:01**	**AQU/AIR**
CRES	Feb 21 2026	01:56	ARI/FIRE
FIRST	Feb 24 2026	12:27	GEM/AIR
GIBB	Feb 27 2026	22:34	CAN/WATER
FULL	**Mar 3 2026**	**11:37**	**VIR/EARTH**
DISS	Mar 7 2026	07:24	SCO/WATER
LAST	Mar 11 2026	09:39	SAG/FIRE
BALS	Mar 15 2026	09:57	AQU/AIR
NEW	Mar 19 2026	01:24	PIS/WATER
CRES	Mar 22 2026	10:27	TAU/EARTH
FIRST	Mar 25 2026	19:18	CAN/WATER
GIBB	Mar 29 2026	08:06	LEO/FIRE
FULL	Apr 2 2026	02:12	LIB/AIR
DISS	Apr 6 2026	02:07	SAG/FIRE
LAST	Apr 10 2026	04:52	CAP/EARTH
BALS	Apr 14 2026	01:30	PIS/WATER
NEW	Apr 17 2026	11:51	ARI/FIRE
CRES	Apr 20 2026	17:31	GEM/AIR
FIRST	Apr 24 2026	02:32	LEO/FIRE
GIBB	Apr 27 2026	18:53	VIR/EARTH
FULL	May 1 2026	17:23	SCO/WATER
DISS	May 5 2026	19:45	CAP/EARTH
LAST	May 9 2026	21:11	AQU/AIR
BALS	May 13 2026	13:32	ARI/FIRE
NEW	May 16 2026	20:01	TAU/EARTH
CRES	May 20 2026	00:23	CAN/WATER
FIRST	May 23 2026	11:11	VIR/EARTH
GIBB	May 27 2026	07:14	LIB/AIR
FULL	May 31 2026	08:45	SAG/FIRE

PHASE	DATE	GMT	SIGN/ELEMENT
DISS	Jun 4 2026	11:30	CAP/EARTH
LAST	Jun 8 2026	10:01	PIS/WATER
BALS	Jun 11 2026	22:25	TAU/EARTH
NEW	Jun 15 2026	02:54	GEM/AIR
CRES	Jun 18 2026	08:06	LEO/FIRE
FIRST	Jun 21 2026	21:56	LIB/AIR
GIBB	Jun 25 2026	21:12	SCO/WATER
FULL	Jun 29 2026	23:57	CAP/EARTH
DISS	Jul 4 2026	00:53	AQU/AIR
LAST	Jul 7 2026	19:29	ARI/FIRE
BALS	Jul 11 2026	05:06	GEM/AIR
NEW	Jul 14 2026	09:43	CAN/WATER
CRES	Jul 17 2026	17:35	VIR/EARTH
FIRST	Jul 21 2026	11:06	LIB/AIR
GIBB	Jul 25 2026	12:41	SAG/FIRE
FULL	Jul 29 2026	14:36	AQU/AIR
DISS	Aug 2 2026	11:47	PIS/WATER
LAST	Aug 6 2026	02:22	TAU/EARTH
BALS	Aug 9 2026	10:49	CAN/WATER
NEW	**Aug 12 2026**	**17:37**	**LEO/FIRE**
CRES	Aug 16 2026	05:28	LIB/AIR
FIRST	Aug 20 2026	02:47	SCO/WATER
GIBB	Aug 24 2026	05:22	CAP/EARTH
FULL	**Aug 28 2026**	**04:19**	**PIS/WATER**
DISS	Aug 31 2026	20:32	ARI/FIRE
LAST	Sep 4 2026	07:51	GEM/AIR
BALS	Sep 7 2026	16:59	LEO/FIRE
NEW	Sep 11 2026	03:27	VIR/EARTH
CRES	Sep 14 2026	20:02	SCO/WATER
FIRST	Sep 18 2026	20:44	SAG/FIRE
GIBB	Sep 22 2026	22:34	AQU/AIR
FULL	Sep 26 2026	16:49	ARI/FIRE
DISS	Sep 30 2026	04:01	TAU/EARTH
LAST	Oct 3 2026	13:24	CAN/WATER

PHASE	DATE	GMT	SIGN/ELEMENT	PHASE	DATE	GMT	SIGN/ELEMENT
BALS	Oct 7 2026	00:44	LEO/FIRE	FIRST	Feb 14 2027	07:59	TAU/EARTH
NEW	Oct 10 2026	15:50	LIB/AIR	GIBB	Feb 17 2027	17:18	CAN/WATER
CRES	Oct 14 2026	13:15	SAG/FIRE	**FULL**	**Feb 20 2027**	**23:23**	**VIR/EARTH**
FIRST	Oct 18 2026	16:13	CAP/EARTH	DISS	Feb 24 2027	09:24	LIB/AIR
GIBB	Oct 22 2026	15:20	PIS/WATER	LAST	Feb 28 2027	05:17	SAG/FIRE
FULL	Oct 26 2026	04:11	TAU/EARTH				
DISS	Oct 29 2026	11:24	GEM/AIR	BALS	Mar 4 2027	08:34	CAP/EARTH
				NEW	Mar 8 2027	09:30	PIS/WATER
LAST	Nov 1 2026	20:29	LEO/FIRE	CRES	Mar 12 2027	03:40	TAU/EARTH
BALS	Nov 5 2026	11:02	VIR/EARTH	FIRST	Mar 15 2027	16:24	GEM/AIR
NEW	Nov 9 2026	07:02	SCO/WATER	GIBB	Mar 19 2027	01:44	LEO/FIRE
CRES	Nov 13 2026	08:34	CAP/EARTH	FULL	Mar 22 2027	10:43	LIB/AIR
FIRST	Nov 17 2026	11:48	AQU/AIR	DISS	Mar 26 2027	01:09	SCO/WATER
GIBB	Nov 21 2026	06:43	ARI/FIRE	LAST	Mar 30 2027	00:54	CAP/EARTH
FULL	Nov 24 2026	14:54	GEM/AIR				
DISS	Nov 27 2026	19:56	CAN/WATER	BALS	Apr 3 2027	03:50	AQU/AIR
				NEW	Apr 6 2027	23:51	ARI/FIRE
LAST	Dec 1 2026	06:09	VIR/EARTH	CRES	Apr 10 2027	12:40	GEM/AIR
BALS	Dec 5 2026	00:30	LIB/AIR	FIRST	Apr 13 2027	22:56	CAN/WATER
NEW	Dec 9 2026	00:52	SAG/FIRE	GIBB	Apr 17 2027	09:30	VIR/EARTH
CRES	Dec 13 2026	04:39	AQU/AIR	FULL	Apr 20 2027	22:27	SCO/WATER
FIRST	Dec 17 2026	05:43	PIS/WATER	DISS	Apr 24 2027	17:49	SAG/FIRE
GIBB	Dec 20 2026	20:10	TAU/EARTH	LAST	Apr 28 2027	20:18	AQU/AIR
FULL	Dec 24 2026	01:28	CAN/WATER				
DISS	Dec 27 2026	06:24	LEO/FIRE	BALS	May 2 2027	20:30	PIS/WATER
LAST	Dec 30 2026	19:00	LIB/AIR	NEW	May 6 2027	10:58	TAU/EARTH
				CRES	May 9 2027	19:33	CAN/WATER
BALS	Jan 3 2027	17:09	SCO/WATER	FIRST	May 13 2027	04:44	LEO/FIRE
NEW	Jan 7 2027	20:25	CAP/EARTH	GIBB	May 16 2027	17:31	LIB/AIR
CRES	Jan 11 2027	23:32	PIS/WATER	FULL	May 20 2027	10:59	SCO/WATER
FIRST	Jan 15 2027	20:35	ARI/FIRE	DISS	May 24 2027	10:53	CAP/EARTH
GIBB	Jan 19 2027	07:36	GEM/AIR	LAST	May 28 2027	13:58	PIS/WATER
FULL	Jan 22 2027	12:17	LEO/FIRE				
DISS	Jan 25 2027	19:00	VIR/EARTH	BALS	Jun 1 2027	09:57	ARI/FIRE
LAST	Jan 29 2027	10:56	SCO/WATER	NEW	Jun 4 2027	19:40	GEM/AIR
				CRES	Jun 8 2027	01:36	LEO/FIRE
BALS	Feb 2 2027	12:20	SAG/FIRE	FIRST	Jun 11 2027	10:56	VIR/EARTH
NEW	**Feb 6 2027**	**15:56**	**AQU/AIR**	GIBB	Jun 15 2027	02:42	SCO/WATER
CRES	Feb 10 2027	15:27	ARI/FIRE	FULL	Jun 19 2027	00:45	SAG/FIRE

PHASE	DATE	GMT	SIGN/ELEMENT
DISS	Jun 23 2027	03:35	AQU/AIR
LAST	Jun 27 2027	04:55	ARI/FIRE
BALS	Jun 30 2027	20:30	TAU/EARTH
NEW	Jul 4 2027	03:02	CAN/WATER
CRES	Jul 7 2027	07:58	VIR/EARTH
FIRST	Jul 10 2027	18:39	LIB/AIR
GIBB	Jul 14 2027	14:01	SAG/FIRE
FULL	**Jul 18 2027**	**15:45**	**CAP/EARTH**
DISS	Jul 22 2027	18:57	PIS/WATER
LAST	Jul 26 2027	16:55	TAU/EARTH
BALS	Jul 30 2027	05:03	GEM/AIR
NEW	**Aug 2 2027**	**10:05**	**LEO/FIRE**
CRES	Aug 5 2027	15:35	VIR/EARTH
FIRST	Aug 9 2027	04:54	SCO/WATER
GIBB	Aug 13 2027	04:04	CAP/EARTH
FULL	**Aug 17 2027**	**07:29**	**AQU/AIR**
DISS	Aug 21 2027	08:20	ARI/FIRE
LAST	Aug 25 2027	02:28	GEM/AIR
BALS	Aug 28 2027	12:27	CAN/WATER
NEW	Aug 31 2027	17:40	VIR/EARTH
CRES	Sep 4 2027	01:21	LIB/AIR
FIRST	Sep 7 2027	18:32	SAG/FIRE
GIBB	Sep 11 2027	20:46	AQU/AIR
FULL	Sep 15 2027	23:04	PIS/WATER
DISS	Sep 19 2027	19:42	TAU/EARTH
LAST	Sep 23 2027	10:21	CAN/WATER
BALS	Sep 26 2027	19:38	LEO/FIRE
NEW	Sep 30 2027	02:35	LIB/AIR
CRES	Oct 3 2027	14:05	SCO/WATER
FIRST	Oct 7 2027	11:48	CAP/EARTH
GIBB	Oct 11 2027	15:13	PIS/WATER
FULL	Oct 15 2027	13:47	ARI/FIRE
DISS	Oct 19 2027	05:32	GEM/AIR
LAST	Oct 22 2027	17:28	CAN/WATER
BALS	Oct 26 2027	03:18	VIR/EARTH

PHASE	DATE	GMT	SIGN/ELEMENT
NEW	Oct 29 2027	13:37	SCO/WATER
CRES	Nov 2 2027	06:17	SAG/FIRE
FIRST	Nov 6 2027	08:00	AQU/AIR
GIBB	Nov 10 2027	10:00	ARI/FIRE
FULL	Nov 14 2027	03:26	TAU/EARTH
DISS	Nov 17 2027	14:38	CAN/WATER
LAST	Nov 21 2027	00:48	LEO/FIRE
BALS	Nov 24 2027	12:21	LIB/AIR
NEW	Nov 28 2027	03:25	SAG/FIRE
CRES	Dec 2 2027	01:41	CAP/EARTH
FIRST	Dec 6 2027	05:22	PIS/WATER
GIBB	Dec 10 2027	03:48	TAU/EARTH
FULL	Dec 13 2027	16:09	GEM/AIR
DISS	Dec 16 2027	23:46	LEO/FIRE
LAST	Dec 20 2027	09:11	VIR/EARTH
BALS	Dec 23 2027	23:39	SCO/WATER
NEW	Dec 27 2027	20:13	CAP/EARTH
CRES	Dec 31 2027	22:45	AQU/AIR
FIRST	Jan 5 2028	01:41	ARI/FIRE
GIBB	Jan 8 2028	19:46	GEM/AIR
FULL	**Jan 12 2028**	**04:02**	**CAN/WATER**
DISS	Jan 15 2028	09:26	VIR/EARTH
LAST	Jan 18 2028	19:26	LIB/AIR
BALS	Jan 22 2028	13:52	SAG/FIRE
NEW	**Jan 26 2028**	**15:13**	**AQU/AIR**
CRES	Jan 30 2028	19:09	PIS/WATER
FIRST	Feb 3 2028	19:11	TAU/EARTH
GIBB	Feb 7 2028	09:21	CAN/WATER
FULL	Feb 10 2028	15:04	LEO/FIRE
DISS	Feb 13 2028	19:54	LIB/AIR
LAST	Feb 17 2028	08:08	SCO/WATER
BALS	Feb 21 2028	06:50	CAP/EARTH
NEW	Feb 25 2028	10:38	PIS/WATER
CRES	Feb 29 2028	12:51	ARI/FIRE

PHASE	DATE	GMT	SIGN/ELEMENT
FIRST	Mar 4 2028	09:03	GEM/AIR
GIBB	Mar 7 2028	20:17	LEO/FIRE
FULL	Mar 11 2028	01:05	VIR/EARTH
DISS	Mar 14 2028	07:23	SCO/WATER
LAST	Mar 17 2028	23:23	SAG/FIRE
BALS	Mar 22 2028	01:25	AQU/AIR
NEW	Mar 26 2028	04:32	ARI/FIRE
CRES	Mar 30 2028	02:55	TAU/EARTH
FIRST	Apr 2 2028	19:16	CAN/WATER
GIBB	Apr 6 2028	04:43	VIR/EARTH
FULL	Apr 9 2028	10:27	LIB/AIR
DISS	Apr 12 2028	20:11	SAG/FIRE
LAST	Apr 16 2028	16:37	CAP/EARTH
BALS	Apr 20 2028	19:54	PIS/WATER
NEW	Apr 24 2028	19:47	TAU/EARTH
CRES	Apr 28 2028	13:30	GEM/AIR
FIRST	May 2 2028	02:26	LEO/FIRE
GIBB	May 5 2028	11:23	LIB/AIR
FULL	May 8 2028	19:49	SCO/WATER
DISS	May 12 2028	10:30	CAP/EARTH
LAST	May 16 2028	10:43	AQU/AIR
BALS	May 20 2028	12:55	ARI/FIRE
NEW	May 24 2028	08:17	GEM/AIR
CRES	May 27 2028	21:21	CAN/WATER
FIRST	May 31 2028	07:37	VIR/EARTH
GIBB	Jun 3 2028	17:25	LIB/AIR
FULL	Jun 7 2028	06:08	SAG/FIRE
DISS	Jun 11 2028	02:07	AQU/AIR
LAST	Jun 15 2028	04:28	PIS/WATER
BALS	Jun 19 2028	03:51	TAU/EARTH
NEW	Jun 22 2028	18:28	CAN/WATER
CRES	Jun 26 2028	03:27	LEO/FIRE
FIRST	Jun 29 2028	12:11	LIB/AIR
GIBB	Jul 3 2028	00:21	SCO/WATER
FULL	**Jul 6 2028**	**18:11**	**CAP/EARTH**

PHASE	DATE	GMT	SIGN/ELEMENT
LAST	Jul 14 2028	20:57	ARI/FIRE
BALS	Jul 18 2028	16:45	GEM/AIR
NEW	**Jul 22 2028**	**03:02**	**CAN/WATER**
CRES	Jul 25 2028	08:59	VIR/EARTH
FIRST	Jul 28 2028	17:40	SCO/WATER
GIBB	Aug 1 2028	09:27	SAG/FIRE
FULL	Aug 5 2028	08:10	AQU/AIR
DISS	Aug 9 2028	10:50	ARI/FIRE
LAST	Aug 13 2028	11:46	TAU/EARTH
BALS	Aug 17 2028	03:52	CAN/WATER
NEW	Aug 20 2028	10:43	LEO/FIRE
CRES	Aug 23 2028	15:12	LIB/AIR
FIRST	Aug 27 2028	01:36	SAG/FIRE
GIBB	Aug 30 2028	21:41	CAP/EARTH
FULL	Sep 3 2028	23:48	PIS/WATER
DISS	Sep 8 2028	02:31	TAU/EARTH
LAST	Sep 12 2028	00:46	GEM/AIR
BALS	Sep 15 2028	13:33	LEO/FIRE
NEW	Sep 18 2028	18:24	VIR/EARTH
CRES	Sep 21 2028	23:23	SCO/WATER
FIRST	Sep 25 2028	13:10	CAP/EARTH
GIBB	Sep 29 2028	13:14	AQU/AIR
FULL	Oct 3 2028	16:25	ARI/FIRE
DISS	Oct 7 2028	17:05	TAU/EARTH
LAST	Oct 11 2028	11:57	CAN/WATER
BALS	Oct 14 2028	22:13	VIR/EARTH
NEW	Oct 18 2028	02:57	LIB/AIR
CRES	Oct 21 2028	10:40	SAG/FIRE
FIRST	Oct 25 2028	04:53	AQU/AIR
GIBB	Oct 29 2028	07:30	PIS/WATER
FULL	Nov 2 2028	09:18	TAU/EARTH
DISS	Nov 6 2028	06:13	GEM/AIR
LAST	Nov 9 2028	21:25	LEO/FIRE
BALS	Nov 13 2028	06:29	LIB/AIR
NEW	Nov 16 2028	13:17	SCO/WATER

PHASE	DATE	GMT	SIGN/ELEMENT	PHASE	DATE	GMT	SIGN/ELEMENT
CRES	Nov 20 2028	01:39	CAP/EARTH	FULL	Mar 30 2029	02:26	LIB/AIR
FIRST	Nov 24 2028	00:15	PIS/WATER				
GIBB	Nov 28 2028	03:20	ARI/FIRE	DISS	Apr 2 2029	07:00	SCO/WATER
				LAST	Apr 5 2029	19:52	CAP/EARTH
FULL	Dec 2 2028	01:40	GEM/AIR	BALS	Apr 9 2029	18:42	PIS/WATER
DISS	Dec 5 2028	17:48	CAN/WATER	NEW	Apr 13 2029	21:40	ARI/FIRE
LAST	Dec 9 2028	05:39	VIR/EARTH	CRES	Apr 17 2029	23:38	GEM/AIR
BALS	Dec 12 2028	15:09	SCO/WATER	FIRST	Apr 21 2029	19:50	LEO/FIRE
NEW	Dec 16 2028	02:07	SAG/FIRE	GIBB	Apr 25 2029	06:22	VIR/EARTH
CRES	Dec 19 2028	19:57	AQU/AIR	FULL	Apr 28 2029	10:37	SCO/WATER
FIRST	Dec 23 2028	21:45	ARI/FIRE				
GIBB	Dec 27 2028	23:15	TAU/EARTH	DISS	May 1 2029	17:19	SAG/FIRE
FULL	**Dec 31 2028**	**16:49**	**CAN/WATER**	LAST	May 5 2029	09:48	AQU/AIR
				BALS	May 9 2029	11:09	ARI/FIRE
DISS	Jan 4 2029	03:54	LEO/FIRE	NEW	May 13 2029	13:42	TAU/EARTH
LAST	Jan 7 2029	13:27	LIB/AIR	CRES	May 17 2029	12:19	CAN/WATER
BALS	Jan 11 2029	01:08	SAG/FIRE	FIRST	May 21 2029	04:15	VIR/EARTH
NEW	**Jan 14 2029**	**17:25**	**CAP/EARTH**	GIBB	May 24 2029	12:53	LIB/AIR
CRES	Jan 18 2029	16:15	PIS/WATER	FULL	May 27 2029	18:38	SAG/FIRE
FIRST	Jan 22 2029	19:23	TAU/EARTH	DISS	May 31 2029	05:04	CAP/EARTH
GIBB	Jan 26 2029	17:42	GEM/AIR				
FULL	Jan 30 2029	06:03	LEO/FIRE	LAST	Jun 4 2029	01:19	PIS/WATER
				BALS	Jun 8 2029	03:48	TAU/EARTH
DISS	Feb 2 2029	12:59	VIR/EARTH	**NEW**	**Jun 12 2029**	**03:51**	**GEM/AIR**
LAST	Feb 5 2029	21:51	SCO/WATER	CRES	Jun 15 2029	21:42	LEO/FIRE
BALS	Feb 9 2029	13:05	CAP/EARTH	FIRST	Jun 19 2029	09:54	VIR/EARTH
NEW	Feb 13 2029	10:32	AQU/AIR	GIBB	Jun 22 2029	18:24	SCO/WATER
CRES	Feb 17 2029	12:41	ARI/FIRE	**FULL**	**Jun 26 2029**	**03:23**	**CAP/EARTH**
FIRST	Feb 21 2029	15:10	GEM/AIR	DISS	Jun 29 2029	18:23	AQU/AIR
GIBB	Feb 25 2029	09:20	CAN/WATER				
FULL	Feb 28 2029	17:09	VIR/EARTH	LAST	Jul 3 2029	17:58	ARI/FIRE
				BALS	Jul 7 2029	20:00	GEM/AIR
DISS	Mar 3 2029	21:46	LIB/AIR	**NEW**	**Jul 11 2029**	**15:51**	**CAN/WATER**
LAST	Mar 7 2029	07:52	SAG/FIRE	CRES	Jul 15 2029	04:38	VIR/EARTH
BALS	Mar 11 2029	03:06	AQU/AIR	FIRST	Jul 18 2029	14:15	LIB/AIR
NEW	Mar 15 2029	04:19	PIS/WATER	GIBB	Jul 22 2029	00:17	SAG/FIRE
CRES	Mar 19 2029	07:34	TAU/EARTH	FULL	Jul 25 2029	13:36	AQU/AIR
FIRST	Mar 23 2029	07:32	CAN/WATER	DISS	Jul 29 2029	09:18	PIS/WATER
GIBB	Mar 26 2029	21:30	LEO/FIRE	LAST	Aug 2 2029	11:16	TAU/EARTH

PHASE	DATE	GMT	SIGN/ELEMENT
BALS	Aug 6 2029	11:11	GEM/AIR
NEW	Aug 10 2029	01:56	LEO/FIRE
CRES	Aug 13 2029	10:18	LIB/AIR
FIRST	Aug 16 2029	18:55	SCO/WATER
GIBB	Aug 20 2029	07:48	CAP/EARTH
FULL	Aug 24 2029	01:51	PIS/WATER
DISS	Aug 28 2029	01:42	ARI/FIRE
LAST	Sep 1 2029	04:33	GEM/AIR
BALS	Sep 5 2029	00:55	CAN/WATER
NEW	Sep 8 2029	10:45	VIR/EARTH
CRES	Sep 11 2029	16:14	SCO/WATER
FIRST	Sep 15 2029	01:29	SAG/FIRE
GIBB	Sep 18 2029	18:00	AQU/AIR
FULL	Sep 22 2029	16:29	PIS/WATER
DISS	Sep 26 2029	19:12	TAU/EARTH
LAST	Sep 30 2029	20:57	CAN/WATER
BALS	Oct 4 2029	13:01	LEO/FIRE
NEW	Oct 7 2029	19:15	LIB/AIR
CRES	Oct 10 2029	23:50	SAG/FIRE
FIRST	Oct 14 2029	11:09	CAP/EARTH
GIBB	Oct 18 2029	07:32	PIS/WATER
FULL	Oct 22 2029	09:28	ARI/FIRE
DISS	Oct 26 2029	12:50	GEM/AIR
LAST	Oct 30 2029	11:32	LEO/FIRE
BALS	Nov 2 2029	23:47	VIR/EARTH
NEW	Nov 6 2029	04:24	SCO/WATER
CRES	Nov 9 2029	10:07	CAP/EARTH
FIRST	Nov 13 2029	00:35	AQU/AIR
GIBB	Nov 17 2029	00:34	ARI/FIRE
FULL	Nov 21 2029	04:03	TAU/EARTH
DISS	Nov 25 2029	05:18	CAN/WATER
LAST	Nov 28 2029	23:48	VIR/EARTH
BALS	Dec 2 2029	09:36	LIB/AIR
NEW	**Dec 5 2029**	**14:51**	**SAG/FIRE**
CRES	Dec 8 2029	23:28	AQU/AIR

PHASE	DATE	GMT	SIGN/ELEMENT
FIRST	Dec 12 2029	17:50	PIS/WATER
GIBB	Dec 16 2029	20:28	TAU/EARTH
FULL	**Dec 20 2029**	**22:47**	**GEM/AIR**
DISS	Dec 24 2029	19:27	LEO/FIRE
LAST	Dec 28 2029	09:49	LIB/AIR
BALS	Dec 31 2029	19:01	SCO/WATER
NEW	Jan 4 2030	02:50	CAP/EARTH
CRES	Jan 7 2030	15:37	PIS/WATER
FIRST	Jan 11 2030	14:06	ARI/FIRE
GIBB	Jan 15 2030	17:34	GEM/AIR
FULL	Jan 19 2030	15:55	CAN/WATER
DISS	Jan 23 2030	06:58	VIR/EARTH
LAST	Jan 26 2030	18:15	SCO/WATER
BALS	Jan 30 2030	04:27	SAG/FIRE
NEW	Feb 2 2030	16:07	AQU/AIR
CRES	Feb 6 2030	09:53	ARI/FIRE
FIRST	Feb 10 2030	11:50	TAU/EARTH
GIBB	Feb 14 2030	13:36	CAN/WATER
FULL	Feb 18 2030	06:20	LEO/FIRE
DISS	Feb 21 2030	16:21	LIB/AIR
LAST	Feb 25 2030	01:57	SAG/FIRE
BALS	Feb 28 2030	14:19	CAP/EARTH
NEW	Mar 4 2030	06:35	PIS/WATER
CRES	Mar 8 2030	05:16	TAU/EARTH
FIRST	Mar 12 2030	08:48	GEM/AIR
GIBB	Mar 16 2030	06:42	LEO/FIRE
FULL	Mar 19 2030	17:57	VIR/EARTH
DISS	Mar 23 2030	00:29	SCO/WATER
LAST	Mar 26 2030	09:52	CAP/EARTH
BALS	Mar 30 2030	01:05	AQU/AIR
NEW	Apr 2 2030	22:03	ARI/FIRE
CRES	Apr 7 2030	00:25	GEM/AIR
FIRST	Apr 11 2030	02:57	CAN/WATER
GIBB	Apr 14 2030	20:07	VIR/EARTH
FULL	Apr 18 2030	03:20	LIB/AIR

PHASE	DATE	GMT	SIGN/ELEMENT
DISS	Apr 21 2030	08:18	SAG/FIRE
LAST	Apr 24 2030	18:39	AQU/AIR
BALS	Apr 28 2030	13:14	PIS/WATER
NEW	May 2 2030	14:12	TAU/EARTH
CRES	May 6 2030	17:49	CAN/WATER
FIRST	May 10 2030	17:12	LEO/FIRE
GIBB	May 14 2030	06:13	LIB/AIR
FULL	May 17 2030	11:19	SCO/WATER
DISS	May 20 2030	16:26	CAP/EARTH
LAST	May 24 2030	04:58	PIS/WATER
BALS	May 28 2030	03:06	ARI/FIRE
NEW	**Jun 1 2030**	**06:22**	**GEM/AIR**
CRES	Jun 5 2030	08:20	CAN/WATER
FIRST	Jun 9 2030	03:36	VIR/EARTH
GIBB	Jun 12 2030	13:50	SCO/WATER
FULL	**Jun 15 2030**	**18:41**	**SAG/FIRE**
DISS	Jun 19 2030	01:31	AQU/AIR
LAST	Jun 22 2030	17:20	ARI/FIRE
BALS	Jun 26 2030	18:37	TAU/EARTH
NEW	Jun 30 2030	21:35	CAN/WATER
CRES	Jul 4 2030	19:40	LEO/FIRE
FIRST	Jul 8 2030	11:02	LIB/AIR
GIBB	Jul 11 2030	20:02	SAG/FIRE
FULL	Jul 15 2030	02:11	CAP/EARTH
DISS	Jul 18 2030	12:12	PIS/WATER
LAST	Jul 22 2030	08:08	ARI/FIRE
BALS	Jul 26 2030	11:09	GEM/AIR
NEW	Jul 30 2030	11:11	LEO/FIRE
CRES	Aug 3 2030	04:24	VIR/EARTH
FIRST	Aug 6 2030	16:43	SCO/WATER
GIBB	Aug 10 2030	01:52	CAP/EARTH
FULL	Aug 13 2030	10:44	AQU/AIR
DISS	Aug 17 2030	01:16	ARI/FIRE
LAST	Aug 21 2030	01:16	TAU/EARTH

PHASE	DATE	GMT	SIGN/ELEMENT
BALS	Aug 25 2030	03:49	CAN/WATER
NEW	Aug 28 2030	23:07	VIR/EARTH
CRES	Sep 1 2030	11:38	LIB/AIR
FIRST	Sep 4 2030	21:56	SAG/FIRE
GIBB	Sep 8 2030	08:23	AQU/AIR
FULL	Sep 11 2030	21:18	PIS/WATER
DISS	Sep 15 2030	17:06	TAU/EARTH
LAST	Sep 19 2030	19:57	GEM/AIR
BALS	Sep 23 2030	19:47	LEO/FIRE
NEW	Sep 27 2030	09:55	LIB/AIR
CRES	Sep 30 2030	18:34	SCO/WATER
FIRST	Oct 4 2030	03:56	CAP/EARTH
GIBB	Oct 7 2030	16:50	AQU/AIR
FULL	Oct 11 2030	10:47	ARI/FIRE
DISS	Oct 15 2030	11:29	GEM/AIR
LAST	Oct 19 2030	14:51	CAN/WATER
BALS	Oct 23 2030	10:36	VIR/EARTH
NEW	Oct 26 2030	20:16	SCO/WATER
CRES	Oct 30 2030	02:23	SAG/FIRE
FIRST	Nov 2 2030	11:55	AQU/AIR
GIBB	Nov 6 2030	04:21	PIS/WATER
FULL	Nov 10 2030	03:30	TAU/EARTH
DISS	Nov 14 2030	07:07	CAN/WATER
LAST	Nov 18 2030	08:33	LEO/FIRE
BALS	Nov 22 2030	00:10	LIB/AIR
NEW	**Nov 25 2030**	**06:47**	**SAG/FIRE**
CRES	Nov 28 2030	11:46	CAP/EARTH
FIRST	Dec 1 2030	22:57	PIS/WATER
GIBB	Dec 5 2030	19:41	ARI/FIRE
FULL	**Dec 9 2030**	**22:41**	**GEM/AIR**
DISS	Dec 14 2030	02:05	LEO/FIRE
LAST	Dec 18 2030	00:00	VIR/EARTH
BALS	Dec 21 2030	12:24	SCO/WATER
FIRST	Dec 31 2030	13:36	ARI/FIRE

PHASE	DATE	GMT	SIGN/ELEMENT
GIBB	Jan 4 2031	14:30	TAU/EARTH
FULL	Jan 8 2031	18:26	CAN/WATER
DISS	Jan 12 2031	18:45	VIR/EARTH
LAST	Jan 16 2031	12:47	LIB/AIR
BALS	Jan 19 2031	23:05	SAG/FIRE
NEW	Jan 23 2031	04:31	AQU/AIR
CRES	Jan 26 2031	12:52	PIS/WATER
FIRST	Jan 30 2031	07:43	TAU/EARTH
GIBB	Feb 3 2031	11:08	GEM/AIR
FULL	Feb 7 2031	12:46	LEO/FIRE
DISS	Feb 11 2031	08:25	LIB/AIR
LAST	Feb 14 2031	22:50	SCO/WATER
BALS	Feb 18 2031	08:17	CAP/EARTH
NEW	Feb 21 2031	15:49	PIS/WATER
CRES	Feb 25 2031	04:43	ARI/FIRE
FIRST	Mar 1 2031	04:02	GEM/AIR
GIBB	Mar 5 2031	07:20	CAN/WATER
FULL	Mar 9 2031	04:30	VIR/EARTH
DISS	Mar 12 2031	19:09	SCO/WATER
LAST	Mar 16 2031	06:36	SAG/FIRE
BALS	Mar 19 2031	16:26	AQU/AIR
NEW	Mar 23 2031	03:49	ARI/FIRE
CRES	Mar 26 2031	22:14	TAU/EARTH
FIRST	Mar 31 2031	00:32	CAN/WATER
GIBB	Apr 4 2031	01:18	LEO/FIRE
FULL	Apr 7 2031	17:21	LIB/AIR
DISS	Apr 11 2031	03:34	SAG/FIRE
LAST	Apr 14 2031	12:58	CAP/EARTH
BALS	Apr 18 2031	00:35	PIS/WATER
NEW	Apr 21 2031	16:57	TAU/EARTH
CRES	Apr 25 2031	16:20	GEM/AIR
FIRST	Apr 29 2031	19:20	LEO/FIRE
GIBB	May 3 2031	16:16	VIR/EARTH
FULL	**May 7 2031**	**03:40**	**SCO/WATER**

PHASE	DATE	GMT	SIGN/ELEMENT
DISS	May 10 2031	10:26	CAP/WATER
LAST	May 13 2031	19:07	AQU/AIR
BALS	May 17 2031	09:49	ARI/FIRE
NEW	**May 21 2031**	**07:17**	**GEM/AIR**
CRES	May 25 2031	09:45	CAN/WATER
FIRST	May 29 2031	11:20	VIR/EARTH
GIBB	Jun 2 2031	04:19	LIB/AIR
FULL	**Jun 5 2031**	**11:58**	**SAG/FIRE**
DISS	Jun 8 2031	16:43	AQU/AIR
LAST	Jun 12 2031	02:21	PIS/WATER
BALS	Jun 15 2031	21:01	TAU/EARTH
NEW	Jun 19 2031	22:25	GEM/AIR
CRES	Jun 24 2031	01:26	LEO/FIRE
FIRST	Jun 28 2031	00:19	LIB/AIR
GIBB	Jul 1 2031	13:47	SCO/WATER
FULL	Jul 4 2031	19:02	CAP/EARTH
DISS	Jul 7 2031	23:32	PIS/WATER
LAST	Jul 11 2031	11:50	ARI/FIRE
BALS	Jul 15 2031	10:32	GEM/AIR
NEW	Jul 19 2031	13:40	CAN/WATER
CRES	Jul 23 2031	15:01	VIR/EARTH
FIRST	Jul 27 2031	10:35	SCO/WATER
GIBB	Jul 30 2031	21:18	SAG/FIRE
FULL	Aug 3 2031	01:46	AQU/AIR
DISS	Aug 6 2031	08:07	PIS/WATER
LAST	Aug 10 2031	00:24	TAU/EARTH
BALS	Aug 14 2031	02:07	CAN/WATER
NEW	Aug 18 2031	04:32	LEO/FIRE
CRES	Aug 22 2031	02:35	LIB/AIR
FIRST	Aug 25 2031	18:40	SAG/FIRE
GIBB	Aug 29 2031	03:44	CAP/EARTH
FULL	Sep 1 2031	09:21	PIS/WATER
DISS	Sep 4 2031	19:31	ARI/FIRE
LAST	Sep 8 2031	16:15	GEM/AIR

PHASE	DATE	GMT	SIGN/ELEMENT	PHASE	DATE	GMT	SIGN/ELEMENT
BALS	Sep 12 2031	19:11	LEO/FIRE	FIRST	Jan 19 2032	12:14	ARI/FIRE
NEW	Sep 16 2031	18:47	VIR/EARTH	GIBB	Jan 23 2032	10:03	GEM/AIR
CRES	Sep 20 2031	12:32	SCO/WATER	FULL	Jan 27 2032	12:53	LEO/FIRE
FIRST	Sep 24 2031	01:20	CAP/EARTH	DISS	Jan 31 2032	15:44	VIR/EARTH
GIBB	Sep 27 2031	10:09	AQU/AIR				
FULL	Sep 30 2031	18:57	ARI/FIRE	LAST	Feb 4 2032	13:49	SCO/WATER
				BALS	Feb 8 2032	01:57	CAP/EARTH
DISS	Oct 4 2031	10:19	TAU/EARTH	NEW	Feb 11 2032	06:24	AQU/AIR
LAST	Oct 8 2031	10:50	CAN/WATER	CRES	Feb 14 2032	12:07	ARI/FIRE
BALS	Oct 12 2031	12:57	VIR/EARTH	FIRST	Feb 18 2032	03:29	TAU/EARTH
NEW	Oct 16 2031	08:21	LIB/AIR	GIBB	Feb 22 2032	04:34	CAN/WATER
CRES	Oct 19 2031	21:23	SAG/FIRE	FULL	Feb 26 2032	07:43	VIR/EARTH
FIRST	Oct 23 2031	07:37	CAP/EARTH				
GIBB	Oct 26 2031	17:53	PIS/WATER	DISS	Mar 1 2032	07:52	LIB/AIR
FULL	**Oct 30 2031**	**07:33**	**TAU/EARTH**	LAST	Mar 5 2032	01:47	SAG/FIRE
				BALS	Mar 8 2032	11:17	AQU/AIR
DISS	Nov 3 2031	04:19	GEM/AIR	NEW	Mar 11 2032	16:25	PIS/WATER
LAST	Nov 7 2031	07:02	LEO/FIRE	CRES	Mar 15 2032	01:31	TAU/EARTH
BALS	Nov 11 2031	06:39	LIB/AIR	FIRST	Mar 18 2032	20:57	GEM/AIR
NEW	**Nov 14 2031**	**21:09**	**SCO/WATER**	GIBB	Mar 22 2032	23:38	LEO/FIRE
CRES	Nov 18 2031	05:49	CAP/EARTH	FULL	Mar 27 2032	00:46	LIB/AIR
FIRST	Nov 21 2031	14:45	AQU/AIR	DISS	Mar 30 2032	20:28	SCO/WATER
GIBB	Nov 25 2031	04:06	ARI/FIRE				
FULL	Nov 28 2031	23:19	GEM/AIR	LAST	Apr 3 2032	10:10	CAP/EARTH
				BALS	Apr 6 2032	18:47	PIS/WATER
DISS	Dec 3 2031	00:22	CAN/WATER	NEW	Apr 10 2032	02:40	ARI/FIRE
LAST	Dec 7 2031	03:20	VIR/EARTH	CRES	Apr 13 2032	16:24	GEM/AIR
BALS	Dec 10 2031	23:19	SCO/WATER	FIRST	Apr 17 2032	15:25	CAN/WATER
NEW	Dec 14 2031	09:05	SAG/FIRE	GIBB	Apr 21 2032	17:55	VIR/EARTH
CRES	Dec 17 2031	14:35	AQU/AIR	**FULL**	**Apr 25 2032**	**15:10**	**SCO/WATER**
FIRST	Dec 21 2031	00:01	PIS/WATER	DISS	Apr 29 2032	05:35	SAG/FIRE
GIBB	Dec 24 2031	17:33	TAU/EARTH				
FULL	Dec 28 2031	17:33	CAN/WATER	LAST	May 2 2032	16:01	AQU/AIR
				BALS	May 6 2032	01:32	ARI/FIRE
DISS	Jan 1 2032	20:45	LEO/FIRE	**NEW**	**May 9 2032**	**13:36**	**TAU/EARTH**
LAST	Jan 5 2032	22:04	LIB/AIR	CRES	May 13 2032	08:12	CAN/WATER
BALS	Jan 9 2032	13:58	SAG/FIRE	FIRST	May 17 2032	09:44	LEO/FIRE
NEW	Jan 12 2032	20:06	CAP/EARTH	GIBB	May 21 2032	10:21	LIB/AIR
CRES	Jan 16 2032	00:32	PIS/WATER	FULL	May 25 2032	02:37	SAG/FIRE

PHASE	DATE	GMT	SIGN/ELEMENT
DISS	May 28 2032	12:11	CAP/EARTH
LAST	May 31 2032	20:51	PIS/WATER
BALS	Jun 4 2032	08:44	ARI/FIRE
NEW	Jun 8 2032	01:32	GEM/AIR
CRES	Jun 12 2032	00:24	LEO/FIRE
FIRST	Jun 16 2032	03:00	VIR/EARTH
GIBB	Jun 20 2032	00:21	SCO/WATER
FULL	Jun 23 2032	11:33	CAP/EARTH
DISS	Jun 26 2032	17:35	AQU/AIR
LAST	Jun 30 2032	02:12	ARI/FIRE
BALS	Jul 3 2032	17:25	TAU/EARTH
NEW	Jul 7 2032	14:42	CAN/WATER
CRES	Jul 11 2032	16:35	VIR/EARTH
FIRST	Jul 15 2032	18:32	LIB/AIR
GIBB	Jul 19 2032	11:46	SAG/FIRE
FULL	Jul 22 2032	18:52	AQU/AIR
DISS	Jul 25 2032	23:15	PIS/WATER
LAST	Jul 29 2032	09:25	TAU/EARTH
BALS	Aug 2 2032	04:22	GEM/AIR
NEW	Aug 6 2032	05:12	LEO/FIRE
CRES	Aug 10 2032	08:18	LIB/AIR
FIRST	Aug 14 2032	07:51	SCO/WATER
GIBB	Aug 17 2032	21:04	CAP/EARTH
FULL	Aug 21 2032	01:47	AQU/AIR
DISS	Aug 24 2032	06:36	ARI/FIRE
LAST	Aug 27 2032	19:34	GEM/AIR
BALS	Aug 31 2032	18:04	CAN/WATER
NEW	Sep 4 2032	20:57	VIR/EARTH
CRES	Sep 8 2032	22:58	SCO/WATER
FIRST	Sep 12 2032	18:49	SAG/FIRE
GIBB	Sep 16 2032	05:02	AQU/AIR
FULL	Sep 19 2032	09:30	PIS/WATER
DISS	Sep 22 2032	16:36	TAU/EARTH
LAST	Sep 26 2032	09:13	CAN/WATER
BALS	Sep 30 2032	10:38	LEO/FIRE

PHASE	DATE	GMT	SIGN/ELEMENT
NEW	Oct 4 2032	13:26	LIB/AIR
CRES	Oct 8 2032	12:02	SAG/FIRE
FIRST	Oct 12 2032	03:48	CAP/EARTH
GIBB	Oct 15 2032	12:39	PIS/WATER
FULL	**Oct 18 2032**	**18:58**	**ARI/FIRE**
DISS	Oct 22 2032	05:51	GEM/AIR
LAST	Oct 26 2032	02:29	LEO/FIRE
BALS	Oct 30 2032	05:33	VIR/EARTH
NEW	**Nov 3 2032**	**05:45**	**SCO/WATER**
CRES	Nov 6 2032	23:17	CAP/EARTH
FIRST	Nov 10 2032	11:33	AQU/AIR
GIBB	Nov 13 2032	20:53	ARI/FIRE
FULL	Nov 17 2032	06:42	TAU/EARTH
DISS	Nov 20 2032	22:19	CAN/WATER
LAST	Nov 24 2032	22:48	VIR/EARTH
BALS	Nov 29 2032	01:30	LIB/AIR
NEW	Dec 2 2032	20:53	SAG/FIRE
CRES	Dec 6 2032	09:02	CAP/EARTH
FIRST	Dec 9 2032	19:09	PIS/WATER
GIBB	Dec 13 2032	06:26	TAU/EARTH
FULL	Dec 16 2032	20:49	GEM/AIR
DISS	Dec 20 2032	17:31	LEO/FIRE
LAST	Dec 24 2032	20:39	LIB/AIR
BALS	Dec 28 2032	20:37	SCO/WATER